Reviews of the book:

Tony Mann has been facilitating for 19 years. He 'became' a Facilitator by accident and since then has been honing his craft and developing his expertise so that now he is in demand by a diverse range of organisations. He has trained hundreds of managers and Facilitators and change agents in the art, science and skill of facilitation in a wide variety of organisations.

He has created and developed many of the models in this book through his practical real life facilitation experiences. He has also built a body of underpinning knowledge and theory, which managers and Facilitators find especially helpful.

This book pulls this knowledge and practice together to help Facilitators build their expertise.

Facilitation –
An *Art, Science, Skill*
or *all three?*

Build your expertise in Facilitation

Tony Mann

𝒭𝒫

Publishing House

First Published by RP Publishing House in 2007

Discounts on bulk quantities of this book are available to businesses, professional associations and other organisations. For details, contact:
RP Publishing House
Tel: +44 1274 829003
79 – 79A Norman Lane
Bradford
BD2 2JX
Email: sales@resourceproductions.com

Fully revised edition November 2009

British Library Cataloguing in Publication data
Facilitation - an Art, Science or Skill or all three? Build your expertise in Facilitation

Mann, Tony
British Library Cataloguing in Publication Data.
A catalogue record for this book is available from the British Library.

I. Title
ISBN 978 0 9556435 0 7
Printed and bound in Great Britain by
CPI Antony Rowe, Chippenham and Eastbourne

Acknowledgements

This book would never have been written if not for the willingness of managers, co-facilitators and organisations to take on board the concepts and principles espoused in theses pages and to take the risk to try out the different ways of working and use the various tools and techniques.

I also want to acknowledge the many hundreds of managers who have used the Process Iceberg approach to facilitation and believed enough in the methodology to defy gravity and have a go at using it in their organisations.

My particular thanks go to the individuals who encouraged me to write the book and caused me to believe that it had a valid place in the world of facilitation. These people showed their commitment to facilitating in this way and the many others who I hope I have thanked personally.

Finally, my wife Sue who has encouraged me over many years and saw these ideas develop and it is her quiet support that is truly behind this book.

CONTENTS

Introduction

Let me ask you to imagine that you are standing outside the door of a meeting room in any typical organisation. You have been waiting outside for some time – you are keen to speak with one of the people who is inside. After a long delay, 40 minutes in fact, the door opens and people start to emerge. The first thing you notice are their faces and their demeanour. Everyone seems downcast, one looks surly, two look resigned and two disheartened. The person you have come to meet hardly notices you. You wonder what has happened inside the room. Then on another day, you are transported to another organisation. This time people come out of the room just five minutes late. People look upbeat, enthusiastic, energised and with a bounce in their step. Everyone is talking to each other as they emerge and the person you are there to meet greets you. So what was different? What happened that made these two sets of people react differently? Well, your initial thought might be that in the first meeting they were being given bad news and in the second, they were being given a bonus! You would be wrong. What if you were told that they were in fact *both* discussing how to resolve a difficult issue? Given the title and subject of this book, you would then, no doubt, say that it was because the second meeting had a 'facilitator'. What if you were told that you were wrong? Then you might be struggling to find an answer. In fact, it is not that the second meeting had a 'facilitator' as such, rather it's because they had a *process* for exploring the issue. Facilitators are experts in designing, applying and using *process*. This, in fact, means that anyone can facilitate if they understand *process* and how to use it.

This book, then, is all about *process*. It is about the principles and the concepts of *process*, and about the models, tools and techniques that make up *process*. This book will also attempt to destroy the myth that facilitators are born, not made. This should encourage you that, if you give attention to understanding process and how it works, you too could be an excellent facilitator. Have you ever seen a performer keeping plates spinning on top of sticks? They rush round giving each plate a spin before it loses momentum and falls to the ground. Good facilitators do not go round spinning meetings and rescuing them, rather they teach people to understand process and apply it. For instance a public administrator (a civil servant in the UK) learned the basics of process and has been able to apply it to several meetings and get results. The only disappointment is that the skill resides with him. He is just seen as a 'good chair'. Ideally, everyone should recognise what he is doing and be able to do likewise. Unfortunately, the mystique seems to reside in people, rather than in the organisation in becoming process aware. It would be rather odd, would it not, if the team leader or manager, in a bread making or a car-making factory was the *only* one who understood the *process.* It would be so odd as to be ridiculous. How much sillier is it then to have a meeting where no one understands how to deploy a *process* in order to make the meeting produce solutions?

There is one major difference, of course, and that is: bread is bread and a car is a car and once the process has been designed *all* the bread and all the cars will go down the production line and come out the same. I am, in fact, being a bit disingenuous to bread makers because *every* batch of bread is different: different wheat; different moisture content; different live ingredients. Therein lies the clue. Each meeting is different: there are different issues; different people; different aspects to the problem and *each* needs a *different* process. However, the *principles* stay the same. This book examines those principles and, together with a range of tools and techniques, you will learn how to *deploy* them in order to design and facilitate excellent events.

I have been facilitating for nearly twenty years. It seems a long time and at times, I despair at the way we waste so much time in fruitless meetings. In a factory one of the key performance measures is 'wastage' or in food manufacturing 'spillage'. What if there was the same performance measure in producing solutions, in resolving problems, in making key decisions? Most companies would fail miserably in meeting their targets! Yet, we do not see the connection. We abhor wastage in our production processes but allow ourselves huge wastage in meetings. This apparent lack of awareness means that we do not put in the performance improvement actions, which would be second nature in a manufacturing environment.

This book seeks to redress this anomaly. It is designed to provide you as a manager, team leader, specialist, change agent or whatever your role with the means to improve the production of issue resolution, innovative ideas, solutions and decisions.

You may be wondering why I do not mention 'buy-in', 'handling difficult people' or 'conflict resolution'. The reason is that these three things are all managed through the *process* not as separate aspects.

This book will give you insight into the concepts and the principles underpinning process – so that you understand why process is important and what it is. It examines the difference between *what* the group are trying to achieve and *how* the group goes about it. It will provide you with a range of (process) models, tools and techniques and explain how *format* works. It will encourage you to understand people better so that

Introduction

your process fits both the task and the people you have working on it. In the same way as a manufacturing process takes account of the raw materials and the ingredients, so you need to understand people and how they function. Finally, this book will give you the opportunity to practice these skills by doing the exercises and seeking to find effective process to manage the situations described. As an Activist learner, you may well have already tried them out. However, you will find yourself better equipped to make sense of it once you have read this book.

Depending on your Learning Style, you may decide to start reading at any number of different points in the book. Certainly, if you are a Pragmatist Appendix 1 will be where you will want to dip in. If you are a Theorist you will probably prefer to read through from the beginning, in order to first gain a deeper understanding of the principles and underpinning theory, before you look elsewhere in the book. The Activist may start with the exercises and then come back to see what they missed. Reflectors will probably sit and read the book from cover to cover – as always, they will be the ones (together with the theorists) who have embedded the concepts, understood the context and can see how it applies. Their Pragmatist colleagues will join them when they get round to the application.

Throughout the book I talk about *'process'* and *'task'* - *'green'* and *'red'* thinking. It is essential you get hold of these concepts wherever you start in the book. It is also important to treat the book as a whole. The description of each of the models, tools and techniques is only useful if you understand *how* to use them. You need to think about your *role* and, to that end, I use the word 'facilitation/facilitator' when I am talking in the generic sense of someone handling process. I use the word Facilitator (with a capital F) when I am talking about the Facilitator working with a group as *their* Facilitator.

The book explores the art, science and skill of facilitation. It examines each aspect, and suggests that it is the combination of all three of these components which make for effective facilitation. The book explores each of these facets and identifies how the facilitator needs to be artistic in designing good process; scientific in their understanding of time and effort; and skilful in deploying the models, tools and techniques at their disposal.

Finally, enjoy! The book is designed to support your endeavours, to give insight to your trials to date and to help provide a framework for managing more effective interactions in the future whether in a personal journey or an organisational context.

Chapter One – Task and Process and Two Key Tools

Context

This book deals with 'production'. In the Introduction you will have seen how any self respecting manufacturing manager would be appalled at 'wastage' in their production process. In the same way, they are committed to the principle of 'right first time', which means that each product off the production line is defect free. When people like Duran and Deming travelled to Japan after the war and saw Japanese factories producing goods that had no defects they were amazed. When they went back to America with the stories and the methodology to go with it, people thought that they were mad. How could you have zero defects? How could you have everything right first time? How could you run a plant with no quality assurance people – where quality was 'built-in'? Eventually, all manufacturers adopted this thinking and manufacturing production looks very different today from how it did thirty years ago. If you walked down a production line some years ago and you got to the end, you might have seen two or three of the items stacked up in the corner. If you asked why they were there, the manager would probably have said that they were damaged and needed to go back through the production process.

I once visited a small plant making circuit boards for the mobile phone industry and there were piles of discarded boards in the corner. When I asked, the manager said that people had damaged them in the production process by over tightening screws and misaligning the parts.

This would not happen *anywhere* today – or the factory would be taken over and new management would come in to sort it out. Factories rage war on wastage and they continually seek to increase production capacity, that is, getting more from the same resources. This mantra covers *all* types of (manufacturing) production, whether it is cars, food, carpets or washing machines. So what is the lesson for us?

Some eight years ago, I was asked to facilitate a group of people trying to develop a strategy for a particular part of the business. When I asked the background to the situation, people told me that it had been tried before but no one had been able to create an effective strategy. In fact this was the third time a group of managers had tried to tackle it!

Do you see the similarity? This strategy had been down the 'production line' and had come off the end not fit for purpose and needing to be re-worked. Contrast that with a manager who said:

"I've recently been chairing a series of workshops to help start IT development work on schedule and contribute towards developing an operating model for an upcoming change. In chairing the workshops, I put the techniques to good use.

The workshops contained a broad range of stakeholders with diverse views/opinions and it was quite an achievement to arrive at a consensus (albeit with some outstanding issues (there always are though) which we are currently taking forward). The outcome being that we can start IT development work and detailed job design work to the dates currently in our plan as well as getting the operating model closer to sign-off".

There are several key points here:

- he needed to develop 'an operating model for an upcoming change'! So he was producing something. He was managing production. He had workers and needed to get something out of his 'factory'.
- he was using techniques (which are the building blocks of process) to build consensus and develop the aspects of the model.
- he called it a 'workshop'. He might have called it a 'meeting' but somehow you sense that he felt that it was different. Yet this was no 'training' workshop. This was not a lecture or presentation. This was work and it was the proper environment to tackle the issues.
- he was chairing it, not acting as a facilitator, but he was using the tools of the trade.
- there were people with diverse views and opinions. In the same way as a bread manufacturer has to work with different types of wheat and water and different moisture content he had to work with people with different perspectives.
- notice, there were some outstanding issues *"..There always are though..."* Yes, but in modern manufacturing these outstanding problems of wastage and underutilization of resources are gradually eliminated.

Knowing the environment that this person works in, he was very bold to use a workshop format and to employ 'techniques'. However, he was a) tired of failure b) ready for change and c) willing to apply process to his production.

So why is the point here? You need to:
- see *all* times of (management) activity as potentially a *production* matter, whether it be budget setting; problem resolution or innovative thinking.
- recognise that *process* is the key management concept that we have been missing
- see *all interactions* between people as a time when we can utilise this approach.
- reduce *wastage* in 'meetings'.
- improve *productivity* and the use of our (human) resources and time.

For ease of reference the term 'meeting' will be used to represent any format where people are interacting to tackle issues.

Task and Process
The fundamental thing you need to understand is the difference between *task* and *process.* You need to see how these two elements of any meeting or project are symbiotically connected but fundamentally different. The two terms therefore need to be defined.

Task
Task is *what* the group is doing. It is the issue facing them, the item on the agenda, the topic of the workshop. Everyone is familiar with this element. People go into meeting to discuss things; to resolve issues; explore ideas.

Managers give little or no effort to the *process.* In a manufacturing plant the opposite is the case, managers concentrate on the *process.* Their thinking is that if the *process* is working well then the production will go well. Yet in management meetings, the *Task* is the element that managers focus on. Look at the illustration in the Table below:

Speaker	Discussion	Comments	Task	Process
Andrew	"We have to look at cutting costs in the year ahead"	This is a straightforward statement of *Task*	✓	
Fiona	"Well I think there is room for cutting component costs"	This might at first glance look like *process* where as in fact it is a sub element of the *Task*.	✓	

Suchit	"Why are we focusing on components – there are other areas where we could cut costs without compromising quality?"	This is another element which a good facilitator would take note of and build in to their *process* suggestions but it is still *Task*	✓	
Heidi	"I think we need to be careful to avoid a blanket cut which could have drastic effects on certain budgets"	The conversation would go on like this for sometime. Here again this is another 'element' of the *Task* but not *process*	✓	
Gursha	"I think that if we need to cut costs, first we need to identify *all* the potential areas where we might cut costs, because as Suchit said we need to avoid focusing on just one or two areas… perhaps we could **list them all on the flip chart in a column**…"	This is the first attempt at *process.* Gursha has linked the Task with a 'piece' of process. (The process words are highlighted).		✓

Table

Each person is chipping in with other aspects and other elements but no one suggesting *how* to take the task forward. Look at the diagram below. Any objective can be broken down into sub elements, which further delineate the nature of the task.

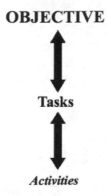

OBJECTIVE

Tasks

Activities

However, this does not constitute *process*. As long as a group is defining the *task*, they are not identifying *how* to tackle it. On the other hand, notice Gursha's interjection. She notices the thread that has been started and offers a 'piece' of process. This is so important.

Take a few moments out next time you are in a meeting, (no one will notice that you have mentally dropped out of the conversation!), watch and listen to people, you will be amazed how much emphasis is on the task and how little attention is given to the process. Much of what people say refines the task and elicits sub elements but this should not be confused with *process*. In the next part of this chapter, we will talk about the nature of the *task* and how difficult it can become, but for now, we need to recognise the *difference* between *task* and *process*.

Process is the means of addressing the *task*, of finding ways to make headway. It offers, just as it does in a manufacturing environment, the means of production. It takes raw materials (ideas and thoughts) and turns them into a finished product with the minimum of waste (effort) and the maximisation of the resources (people's time). That is why it is always such a waste when people sit in a meeting and have nothing to say. They know they do not need to be there and yet they dutifully take their place and contribute nothing. As such, they are wasting valuable resource. Imagine what a factory manager would say if, as they went round the production line, they saw raw materials laying unused (ideas abandoned)! If they saw people doing nothing and waste on the floor (time and energy)! We need to harness *process* in order to have an effective production line.

Process

So what is *process*? Put simply, it is the *means* of production, not the product, nor the raw materials, but it does take raw materials and turn them into finished product. In the same way that if you looked at a production line, you would see machinery which was taking the raw material and turning it into product, so in a meeting, you would see carefully designed pieces of process which were turning the raw material (of ideas and thoughts) into a solution, a decision, an outcome. If you go in a factory you should be amazed at how cleverly designed the machines are. In the same way, you should be able to look into a meeting (room) and see a cleverly designed process that is working to make solutions and decisions.

Understanding Task and Process

TASK = What we do
PROCESS (FORMAT)= How we do it

Therefore there are "Task *issues*"
and
"Process/Format *methods*"

Now, a word of warning. Whilst the general principle of *task* and *process* being linked is true of production in manufacturing and meetings, there is a fundamental difference between a manufacturing process and a meeting process. In manufacturing, the process is *fixed*. Once a stable process has been designed, it runs without interference as long as everything is going well. Nevertheless, in manufacturing the process is established and designed to be fit for the purpose of production. However, in meetings there can be a myriad of tasks to examine, each one different from the other, each requireing a *different* process. So, whilst, in principle the two environments are the same: both involve production, in management meetings we should expect to see different processes in place to tackle different tasks. However, in a sense this is no different to seeing different *lines* in a manufacturing factory producing different products. You would think it crazy if the same process were used to produce jam as was used to produce biscuits. Yet the factory might be producing both.

However, lazy facilitators or facilitators who do not understand process often bring their 'favourite' process and apply it to *different* tasks. This confuses managers and it will not necessarily be fit for purpose.

The most extreme version of this that I have seen was in a Leadership Conference of international managers. The consultant told us before hand that he would tell all the managers to get into pairs and for one of them to talk about something important to them. The other person was not to: speak, nod, affirm, in fact they were to remain still and avoid any reaction. Then he wanted them to swap over and repeat the process (notice the word 'process'). When we asked him what he meant it to achieve he was rather vague. He said that it had been good when he had done it elsewhere! It was months later that one of us saw a TV programme about 'step-families' and the difficulty for everyone when there are 'step' relationships (step-children, step-father etc). The professional counsellor suggested to the family that each person be allowed to speak for two minutes without interruption; challenge; facial reaction or comments. Then they were to swap over. Do you recognise the similarity in the process? However, in this situation it was easy to see why the counsellor was proposing this particular piece of process. It allowed time and allowed the person to get their point of view across uninterrupted. Now do you think that this was the right piece of process to start a Leadership Conference? The managers certainly did not. They were confused and could not see the point of the 'exercise'.

The point is that *each* task and *each element* of the task needs its own purposefully designed piece of process. I call it 'elegant design'. Process should be 'elegant' and 'fit for purpose'. It should be obvious to people why you are suggesting it and it should achieve the (production) goal of producing an outcome. In manufacturing bread for example, the bread does not appear straight away. First of all the dough has to be mixed – one piece of process. Then it has to be 'proved' - another piece of process; then baked to shape – another piece of process and then wrapped – another piece of process. In the same way, each element of an objective, each task, each activity needs it own piece of process to achieve an outcome. One that will lead eventually to a loaf of bread, to a solution or a decision. Look at the diagram below:

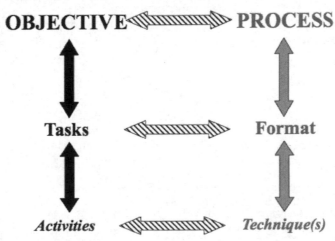

At each level there needs to be a 'piece' of, fit for purpose, process which serves to deliver an outcome in order to achieve a result. In, say, bread production the overall objective is to produce 30,000 loaves of bread and the sub tasks are to make the dough; prove it; bake it; wrap it and load it onto the vehicle. In a management meeting, the overall objective might be as shown below:

Objective: To identify cost savings without risk to quality and safety

Task 1:
   1) Identify any areas where savings might be made
Activities
      1a) Identify aspects of each area where these savings might be made
      1b) Identify the potential savings in monetary terms
Task 2:
   2) Measure each saving against the criteria of risk to: quality and customer satisfaction
Task 3:
   3) Examine any adverse consequences of such cost cutting other than quality and safety (e.g. low morale)

Just as in manufacturing, you can see how an objective might have at least three tasks and a number of sub activities in order to produce a valid and viable solution. Identifying and clarifying the objective; eliciting the tasks and defining the activities in the first part of tackling the issue. The second and equally as important part, and the one often ignored by managers, is designing the process. Let us look at the same example again, this time with the process added:

Task	Process
Objective : To identify cost savings without risk to quality and safety	People say aloud what they think the purpose of the meeting is. This is written on the flip chart and refined as each person speaks until everyone is comfortable with the issue
Task 1:	
Identify any areas where savings might be made	People call out an area and this is written on the flip chart in column 1 of a matrix, until all potential areas have been captured
Activities	
1a) Identify aspects of each area where these	People identify aspects, which could be subject to cost cutting.

savings might be made	
1b) Identify the potential savings in monetary terms	This might mean managers going away and doing some research.
Task 2:	
Measure each saving against the criteria of risk to: quality and customer satisfaction	People then suggest a score for risk against each criteria and everyone challenges or accepts that score. This is done until all the savings have been vetted and an overall risk score is identified.
Task 3:	
Examine any adverse consequences of such cost cutting (other than quality and safety (e.g. low morale)	People brainstorm potential adverse consequences. *(Did you know that as a result of 'speed humps/bumps', the instances of asthma amongst the 'at risk' groups – the young and elderly went up threefold!).*
Task 4:	
The manager's should now be able to articulate areas (and aspects) where cuts could be made	Propose which aspects to apply the cuts and come to agreement.

This symbiotic relationship between *task* and *process* is crucial for effective production. The task needs to be clearly articulated and the process needs to be designed and applied to ensure a good result. It is a crime against good sense to bring in pieces of process which have been used elsewhere but which do not fit the task, no matter how good they look or how much you may like them. In the apocryphal story of Japanese manufacturing, when there is a problem the workers stop the production line and a team of process engineers come and sort out the problem. In the same way, in management meetings if the 'production' is not going well then the team need to stop the meeting and change/adapt the process to achieve the production goal. Teams that have the confidence to identify the objective; articulate the tasks and activities and *then* introduce effective process; use the right format and apply the right techniques will find their productivity improves; their wastage is reduced - their use of resources is maximised and the quality of their management actions will increase markedly.

Red and Green Thinking and Facilitation

In order to teach people to differentiate between task and process it is helpful to use the concept of *task* being *red* thinking and *process* being *green* thinking, for no other reason than they are different colours. It helps separate. In fact, whenever these principles are cascaded across an organisation, one of the concepts that managers insist should be taught is red and green thinking and the difference between the two. Somehow, by giving them colours, people recognise them as different and begin to realise that they are both important and both depend on each other. You cannot deploy process without an appropriate task (as you saw in the example of the Leadership Conference) and you need process to tackle difficult issues (tasks), as illustrated in the example of cutting costs. So from now on in this book reference will be made to 'red' and 'green' thinking. This leads to another principle. There needs to be clarity between the two – between 'red' and 'green'. Ideally, as in manufacturing, the two would run in parallel. However, in a manufacturing plant, the managers monitor the process and that takes care of the production. In management (production) meetings, however, the issues vary, they present themselves differently each time and they require different applications of green thinking. This is where we get the concept of 'facilitation'. It is the facilitator who monitors and oversees the process, the green thinking. It is they who suggest process and offer it to the group. Ideally, the group would manage both. Indeed just as Deming and Duran found when they came back from Japan, people have such a problem accepting the need for process that they almost need someone to 'guard' the green thinking and make sure people remember it!

TASK = TASK LEADER
PROCESS = FACILITATOR

Their respective roles are therefore:

"Task *issues*"
and
"Process *methods*"

Therefore, the facilitator is a 'green' person. They are concerned with selecting process to go with the task. In the example above it may have been that Gursha was the Facilitator, interjecting into the group's discussion and thinking a way of of tackling the task. That or the group was very process aware and someone was 'guarding' the need to find an effective process to take the task forward. Groups do find it difficult to keep swapping from red to green thinking and often it is better, in the early days, to have someone who is committed to green thinking and focuses on that and that alone. This leads us to the next principle, that the facilitator, if there is one, should not get involved in the red discussion. They will of course consider it when they are proposing process but, as a principle, a facilitator is there purely in a green capacity.

I was speaking in New Zealand once and two facilitators commented to each other that the recent assignment had been difficult for exactly that reason. The client had asked them to facilitate some workshop groups discussing and engaging with a new policy. Unfortunately, when questions were raised by members of the group about the efficacy of the policy, the Facilitators were left to give answers and justify the rationale. They realised how this had compromised their position, and their role, and made it difficult for them to offer process. There was the underlying suspicion that the process was designed to get the answer that the Facilitators wanted. It would have been better to have had a 'red' person in the room, who could have dealt with the red questions and left the Facilitators to handle and propose the best process.

I was asked once to facilitate a presentation of 'bad news' to a group of staff. My contract with the leader was that he would take all the 'red' issues and I would find a 'green' way of tackling them. Whilst the session was not a happy one, people felt that their concerns had been heard and handled. The leader felt that he had been able to focus on his answers and what the group was saying to him. In this instance a Facilitator, someone who solely focuses on the 'green', can be invaluable. On other occasions, my role has been to concentrate on designing a process whilst the managers concentrated all of their thinking on the 'red' issues. Even if there is no facilitator, the team should also focus on the green as well as the red because, as we have hopefully demonstrated, with effective and purpose designed process the task will be achieved.

Format and Techniques
In good manufacturing plants, they are always looking for improvements to the process but it is not good practice to keep changing it. In management meetings, it is always good to seek to improve the process

but it is NOT good to keep the *same* process regardless of the task. Imagine that you could look through one of those spy holes in the door of different meeting rooms. Then imagine that you looked through that spy hole every time there was a meeting. What you would probably see would be the same people sitting around the same (boardroom) table, in the same seat. If you recorded what you saw and then played it back in fast time people would probably be seated throughout the meeting and you would notice that their heads turned the same way, to talk to the same people. So what would be odd about that you might ask? If you had done the same thing and looked in at a manufacturing line, the answer would be "Nothing!" You would expect the same process to be in place, every time you looked. You might even see a person checking a dial or two at the same time every hour. So what is odd about the management meeting? Well to have the same *process* every time means that they must have been discussing the *same* issue *every* time you looked! Now whilst organisations do have a morning meeting, a 'catch-up' meeting, even the content should be different enough to justify a different *format* and the use of different *techniques* to explore it. If we accept the premise that task and process have a symbiotic relationship, then if the nature of the task changes, so should the format and techniques being deployed.

So what is *format?*

Well 'format' is the way you use the resources in the room. It is the application of people to process. Looking at the diagram below you will see that there are fundamentally four different formats: *All; Group; All to One* and *One to All*.

All — **Each person works on their own doing the activity, using the technique**

Group — **A group works together doing the activity, using the technique**

All to One — **Everyone directs their input to one person who uses the technique**

One to All — **One person does the activity to or on behalf of everyone else**

Good facilitators understand the difference between these four formats. Each has its own strengths and weaknesses, its own advantages and disadvantages. Each of the four different formats will produce a different outcome and either support the process or work against it. Imagine that there is a forceful character in the room. Imagine that they tend to make their view known very early on in the discussion. Then the probability is that they will taint the discussion. Their view may be the one that prevails. If you introduce a new member to the team, someone who is finding their feet, then they may be so intimidated by this person and their views that they feel unwilling to risk putting their perspective forward. Now the dominant person may think that they are serving the group by offering a viewpoint. The fact they may have been the leading figure, the one whose dynamic thoughts drove the business forward, may now have become a hindrance to the group.

The leader may think that their role is to speak up first. They may not know any better. If you are facilitating in such a situation this is a prime case for preventing a *One to All* format. The best format for this situation will be *All* and *Group*. In the event the leader will probably be glad that others were asked to contribute and it will change the nature of the team. It will become much stronger and better decisions will be made.

Each of the different formats has advantages and disadvantages (see diagram below). Selecting the 'right' one will require analysis of the situation: i.e. the level of process awareness of the group and the time available, in order to use the format that suits best.

Format	Advantages	Disadvantages
All	Everyone gets an opportunity to input their ideas/thoughts/ perceptions	It takes more time to collate the input from everyone and 'cluster'/ analyse it
All to One	There is an opportunity to 'bounce' off others thoughts and it takes less time to elicit the thoughts/ideas	The opinion of individuals can be lost and the opinion of one or two people can hold sway
Group	The opinion of different or 'constituencies' can be developed or cross-cutting groups can provide a mix of opinions/perceptions/views	The group format still needs another format to make it effective (e.g. *All*)
One to All	There is the opportunity to save time and effort by getting expert input	If the expert isn't well directed it can turn into a 'solo' self-centred presentation

Imagine now, for a moment, that you are in the meeting room with the team in the example on page 4, discussing the cost cutting. Gursha suggested a process to the group. What *formats* would you suggest to use in each of the different tasks and activities? When you have had time to think you will find a proposed option in Appendix 2 on page 198 together with the rationale.

Format	Rationale
All	This approach is used when: - there are dominant people in the group and you want people to work independently, free of others influence - you want everyone *own* thoughts/ideas/input
All to One	This approach is used when: - you want cross fertilisation of ideas - there is no danger of domination by individuals
Group	This is used when: - there are different constituencies' in the room and you want to reflect their different perspectives.
One to All	This is used when: - there is an expert in the room who can steer the group by giving their expert input (first)

Models, Tools and Techniques

We will cover various different Models, Tools and Techniques in Appendix 1. Suffice here to describe their function. They give action and the means to tackle the task. The selection of the most appropriate one(s) will enhance and enable the group to produce a satisfactory result. Each one should achieve a certain outcome. In exactly the same way as a piece of machinery achieves an outcome. Using the same analogy as a manufacturing plant again, there are major pieces of equipment which process the products (e.g. oven) and smaller pieces which perhaps manipulate the product (wrap the loaf) and still other smaller items which play a key part in monitoring the production (e.g. dials). In the same way in manufacturing a decision, or solving a problem, or creating new solutions there are models which can help (e.g. the Process Iceberg Model – which we will describe in Chapter 5), Tools (e.g. Force Field analysis) and Techniques (e.g. Braindumping with Post Its™). As in a factory, the major equipment (the oven) has dials, so, in the same way the process Models use Tools and Techniques.

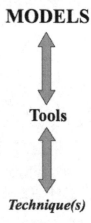

MODELS

Tools

Technique(s)

The Art, Science and Skill of Facilitation

A good facilitator becomes an expert in using these Models, Tools and Techniques and knows when and where to deploy them. They should not have 'favourites', each one should be used as and when they are required. Just as a traditional apprentice learnt how to use the various tools of their trade, so should a facilitator learn how to use the various models, tools and techniques and become familiar with their application. In addition, I believe that a good facilitator can 'hear' the task words, which lead them to use a particular model, tool, or technique. Read the exemplar text below and see what you 'hear':

"I think we need to identify all the issues facing us in this crisis".

"We need to decide which of the cost cutting aspects we should adopt given we don't want to affect customer satisfaction and quantity"

If you can speak "process language" in the same way as you can speak a foreign language then maybe you can interpret what was said above. Interpreting from *'task'* to *'process'*, from *'red'* to *'green'* it might 'sound' something like this:

*"I think we need to (**braindump** all our thoughts and write them on **Post Its**™) to identify all the issues facing us in this crisis".*

*"We need to decide which of the cost cutting aspects (using a **matrix/table** and **score,** each aspect, using points out of, say '5' measuring: customer satisfaction and quality and the ones with the lowest score) we should adopt".*

These are relatively simple examples and yet, like a good apprentice, a good facilitator knows which tool to use in which circumstance. They know their tools and they learn when to use them to best effect. Sometimes they have a choice of tools and sometimes only one will work. You need to attune your brain to hear the green words and filter out the red ones. Here are examples of other Models, Tools and Techniques and the exemplar associated process words associated with them.

Techniques	Situations	Key Words
A Day at the Zoo (Allegory) - see page 137	The task is one that might prove to be emotive for the group. The task is one that will be taken on more successfully if the group can 'distance' itself from the subject matter. *"We have to imagine what this*	*Future/Now How will it be Differently*

	would be like"	
Brain Dumping (a method of collecting data/ information)	It is desirable to draw out from the group all the information that is known about a particular situation, action or event. *"There are a number of factors/issues which we need to explore"*	*Recognise/ identify/find the: Issues Factors Ideas Considerations*
Four Box Model (a means of analysing and sorting data) - see page 131	2 independent factors, each with extremes at each end e.g.*"...It more about cost" ..... "No, to me, its about the benefit"*	*Emotion: disagreement over two different perspectives*
Repertory Grid (a method for collecting data in a complex situation) - see page 140 What will I see Happening a complementary to this Tool (see page 153)	There have been examples of a problem/issue that keep re-occurring. This technique can be used when there are examples of the situation that are 'good' and examples of the situation that are 'poor'. *"But we've got this right before....even if this time we haven't" "Surely it hasn't always been like this?"*	*Good vs Bad Effective vs Not effective Positive experience vs Negative experience*
Process Iceberg® Model/SCA (a Model for analysing situations) – see page 182	This model is best used with SCA as a diagnostic tool. Whenever there are symptoms, the likelihood is that there are causes 'higher up the (Process) Iceberg®. *"Surely we need to change the systems..." "Are we clear why we do this"*	*Any words which reflect the 'hierarchy' of the Process Iceberg®*

SPO

Perhaps this is an appropriate moment to introduce one of the key process tools, which *anyone* can use to link *task* and *process.* It is called SPO. SPO stands for **S**ituation, **P**roposal, **O**utcome/Output (see diagram below). The Situation is a context or background and is a summary of the *task* issues at hand. The Proposal notices this and suggests a *process,* in the form of a model, tool or techniques and format that can be used to tackle the task. The Outcome or output draws this back into the realm of the task and identifies what the group will gain by adopting this way forward.

The SPO is incredibly powerful, for several reasons:
- it connects 'red' and 'green' and makes the symbiotic link
- it demonstrates the significance of 'green' in tackling the task
- it allows the group to take responsibility by enabling people to challenge the S, the P or the O and thus become more aware of process thinking
- it introduces models, tools and techniques *in context* and demonstrates what they are used for
- it gives the facilitator (or anyone) the ability to introduce process

Summarise (the background/context)

Propose (Format, technique(s))

Outcome/Output (what will result)

It connects 'red' and 'green' and makes the symbiotic link
It is essential to emphasis the link between red need and green action and the SPO technique does this. It 'translates' red requirements into a green process and applies the most appropriate model, tool or technique to achieve this.

It demonstrates the significance of 'green' in tackling the task
Consequently, it illustrates the importance of applying green process to achieve outcomes. This is essential when groups are beginning to appreciate the significance of process.

It allows the group to take responsibility by enabling people to challenge the S, the P or the O and thus become more aware of process thinking
Good facilitators demonstrate openly what they are doing. Some readers may remember two magicians: Penn and Teller. Their cleverness was that they did the trick and then showed people *how* they did it. Good facilitators go one-step further and show people *how* to use green *before*

17

they do it. Poor facilitators, or those who are nervous of revealing their expertise, 'do' process but fail to explain the rationale to the group. In order to help a group to mature then it is important that people understand what is happening and why. Offering process, in the form of an SPO, allows the group to challenge that rationale: they might not see the Situation or background in the same way – in which case the (process) proposal will not fit. Someone might be able to refine the Proposal and thus add value and make it even more effective. The group may decide, either, that the proposed model, tool, technique will not do what was promised, or that it is not the Outcome it desires or needs. In which case the group protects itself from wasting time and effort. No one in their right mind would waste raw materials (in a factory) pushing them down the production line if the process was not going to deliver, or was going to produce poor quality goods at the end. It should be the same in a meeting: you need the best possible process to reach the desired outcome.

It introduces models, tools and techniques in context and demonstrates what they are used for
The use of the SPO technique links techniques and tools to the task and illustrates clearly which tool fits best and will give the best outcome. In the same way as a craftsman selects the 'right' tool for the job, so a good facilitator is able to select the right technique/tool *and* demonstrate to the group that it will give the desired outcome. This builds awareness amongst the group that will enable people, by proxy, to understand the use of techniques and tools. Remember the example (on page 6) of the consultant at the Leadership Conference who used a tool without it being connected to the task? Groups need to learn how to connect task and process and the SPO teaches which technique works best in which situation.

It gives the facilitator (or anyone) the ability to introduce process
Consultants and trainers have the right, by virtue of their role, to make suggestions to a group without justification. A trainer who told a group to break into three sub groups would never be questioned or challenged because they have 'control' of the task (and the process). However, facilitators only have 'control' of the process and need to legitimise its process. Their authority comes not from their position; rather it comes from the effective deployment of the best technique or tool to move the task forward.

Practice using the SPO whenever you can and whenever you see the need for process. Practice using it to expand the objective and uncover tasks and activities which make up the objective. For example:

(S) "If we are going to agree a budget for next year ...I think we need to avoid just repeating this year's figures plus or minus 10%. The danger if we do that is we may not be using the finance we have wisely. For example, is our vehicle fleet giving us the flexibility in delivery we need? Is our distribution network effective? (P) I suggest that we need to identify 'value for money' for each element in this current budget. (O) I know this will take time but it will give us a real sense of what is working and what needs adjusting/changing before we set the numbers in place."

You may want to practice at home!
(S) "I'm exhausted from a long day and I imagine that you are too? (P) Why don't we go out for a meal tonight (rather than at the weekend) (O) and that way we will relax and not have to do the dishes afterwards?"

Even try it out in a meeting!
(S) "It seems to me that we are floundering around trying to make sense of this issue and none of us has the depth of experience, we need to understand the essentials. (P) Why don't we put it on next week's agenda and get José from our Spanish office to come over and give us a presentation on the key factors of the European sales effort. (O) That way we don't waste time and it will give us a chance to see José and assess his grip on the issues and the market?"

Many managers have found that by adopting the SPO it has helped broaden their management style. Whereas before they were somewhat dictatorial, the use of the SPO has given the opportunity for the staff to challenge and to provide opportunity for participation. It also makes the manager more thoughtful if they have to justify the S and the O of their Proposal.

Degrees of Uncertainty
When we talk about *task,* there is a tendency to think that all tasks are the same. In one sense, you know that they are not. However, you would be forgiven for thinking they are when you see groups using the same format to tackle each item on the agenda. How can they be different if we are able to use the same process for each? We need to differentiate between such tasks as information giving; decision-making; problem solving and innovation. Yet there is a more subtle difference between tasks, one which we need to examine. This distinction relates to the *Degree of Uncertainty* of the objective.

Certainty

There is a tendency for groups to think that *all* objectives are 'certain'. We tend to approach them as if the question was well defined and the answer was easily identified. This may be so in a small number of cases. However, in the modern business world and in organisations this is hardly ever the case. The great mistake in imagining that objectives are 'certain' is that we do not apply the right process to tackle them. Imagine someone who had been pruning the bushes in their garden and then you saw them using the same pruning tool trying to cut down a tree! You would think that they were mad!

Certainty	**the Question is clear & the answer is easily obtained from the people in the group**
Complexity	**the Question/Problem is relatively clear but the solution has to be developed**
Uncertainty	**Even the nature of the Question/ Problem/Issue is unclear and has to be defined and clarified. Only then can a solution be explored**

However, that is exactly what some management teams do! They try to use tools and techniques, which are only useful in certainty, and by dint of discussion they hope to chop down the tree – or at least prune the offending branches!

Complexity

More often than not, the objective is at least *complex.* We may know the issue and we may be agreed about the question we are asking but we need to identify options, in terms of the solution, and *then* decide the *best* solution in the circumstances. We have already mentioned the case of 'speed bumps' solving one problem and yet creating a new one of increased asthma. There was a famous case of a butter manufacturer who increased the size of the pallets holding the butter because this made the task of offloading wholesale packs easier, more efficient and less costly in time. What they had forgotten was that the mass of butter being put through the deep freeze was now greater and the freezer could not get the centre of the pallet frozen. Consequently, customers complained that their deliveries were rancid on arrival! In another situation, a marketing team came up with the great promotional idea of having a token in a loaf of bread. Just like Willy Wonker, one lucky person would get the winning token. It seemed a great idea until the factories asked *how* they were meant to get the token *inside* the packaging. The wrapping process was automatic and it would require human intervention to put anything *inside* it. The marketing team suggested that managers could re-open the packaging and 'put' the tokens in! Apart from hygiene, the factory managers thought it ludicrous that managers would secretly open a loaf and push tokens inside! The great promotion never happened. Complexity is about identifying the real issue, finding potential solutions and then picking the *most* appropriate one without adverse consequences.

Uncertainty

There are occasions when a group will not even know the question is growing. As strange as it may seem there are many times when we think we know the problem only to find that we were focusing on the wrong question. This means that we have to *find* the issue, determine what the right question is – even before we attempt to identify solutions! Management teams that race ahead and find answers, often discover instead that they have answered the wrong question. A management team at a large leisure centre was troubled by youths invading the five-a-side football pitches. Legitimate players would pay only to find youths on the pitch. The manager would then have the unenviable task of trying to evict them. The meeting began to discuss how the duty manager could handle the situation. Suggestions were made about 'customer care' and 'influencing and assertiveness' courses. Then someone asked what was the real problem. After a while, the group agreed it was the fact that the vandals were *on the* court, not that they had to be persuaded to *get off*! Therefore, the group looked at how to ensure that *only* legitimate people *could* use the courts. Given this new focus and the introduction of techniques like Brainstorming and Re-statement, the group came up with the ingenious plan to have a steal hawser stretched from one end of the pitch to the other so that no one could run across it. The legitimate customer would be given a key to unlock the padlock and release the hawser. This dissuaded the youths from even attempting to play and the problem went away!

One of the problems in 'Uncertainty', which by definition is when you cannot even define the question, is that the very nature of the words we use change their meaning. The very descriptions people try to give things do not have any relevance because you do not yet know what you are defining. If you start saying 'We have to agree a budget for this' the problem is that you don't know what a 'budget' is going to look like until you know what 'this' is. Therefore, to talk about defining a 'budget' has no meaning. A 'budget' in the normal circumstances of 'Certainty': 'I know

21

the question'; 'I know how many sales I've got to make'; 'I know what time-scale I've got to do it in' is not appropriate. Similarly, to imagine you know: 'I need these resources'; 'therefore I need this budget' is not relevant. When you are working in 'Uncertainty' somebody will have to say to you 'What you're saying is we have to at some point define all the resources and all the things that will be needed to make this thing happen'. The person will say something like 'Well, yes, I am, I was using 'budget' in the loosest sense of a mechanism of describing we have to resource this.' Therefore, effective interpersonal skills depend a great deal on the ability to use the language to its best, but also to overcome the inadequacies of the language. In Greek, there are at least four descriptions for 'fire' (as in firing a weapon); there is 'fire when I tell you'. 'fire when you are ready', 'fire and carry on shooting' and then 'fire and then stop'. Consequently, when you say 'fire' in Greek it will be very clear which 'fire' you mean because of the word you choose. However, if you say 'fire' in English, you have to add additional words to make any sense of it. Similarly, in 'Uncertainty' you need to be very careful that the words themselves do not become a problem. People tend to try to define the situation before it is possible to define it, or to use the word in one way and find that another person is using it in another way. Therefore, the responsibility of the facilitator is to give a robust format and to help people to explore the language they are using.

If the Task Leader or the Facilitator suspects that the objective is *uncertain,* the Facilitator should invite anyone to feedback *what they think the objective is.* They then write this on the flip chart in *double spacing.* The Facilitator then invites 'anyone' to say what *they think the objective is.* If it is very similar to the first description then the Facilitator simply writes the additional/different words above the previous ones and reads out the combined statement. They then ask 'someone' else to define the objective and IF the wording is similar, then the objective is 'robust'. IF, however, the words change and the whole meaning is different *each* time someone says it then the Facilitator needs to break the group into pairs/trios and ask them to brain dump the *issues* that pertain to the potential objective. The reason for *Group* is to get maximum participation with maximum opportunity to 'find' the objective. When everyone has had enough time to 'cluster' their thoughts they should be invited to create a 'model'; an analysis of their thinking, and then each group should display their conclusions. The Facilitator can either ask everyone to walk round and view the outputs (*All*), or get each group in turn to present (*One to All*). Then the Facilitator needs to encourage the groups to look for common features of the displays and build a common objective.

Now the real problem with handling: certainty, complexity and uncertainty is the *time* element. Groups do not recognise the time implications of the different scenarios. Here we see an element of mathematics and the 'science' of facilitation. The time required to tackle complexity and uncertainty is far greater than a group would imagine.

Certainty $\qquad$ T = T

Complexity $\qquad$ T = T x 2½

Uncertainty $\quad$ T = T x 4½

Teams and groups are usually experienced enough to recognise the time it takes to tackle *certainty* – T = T. Where 'T' is the time they assess they will need. So if the team sets aside 30 minutes for the task and it is 'certain', then it should take 30 minutes. However, more often than not a chair of a meeting will allocate 30 minutes for an item on the agenda and it will take 75 minutes. That is because it was *complex.* It will take 2½ times *the time that the group imagined it would take.*

Working in *uncertainty* takes even longer. There is a case of a food manufacturer designing, creating and producing a range of luxury cakes, which never sold because the intended customers saw them as unsuitable and inappropriate for them. How many wasted weeks in design and how much wasted production time, let alone the cost of re-tooling to produce the product. Unfortunately, groups that do not recognise and assume uncertainty actually waste all that time finding the wrong answers. A management team *might* realise that 135 minutes, or 2 hours 15 minutes later that they had been in uncertainty. However, in many cases it is weeks or months later that they realise that all their work was wasted. By then people have been deployed doing the wrong thing and the problem has to be re-examined with less energy this time and probably more problems, ones created because of the poor decision from the first attempt.

The most useful thing anyone can do is assess whether the objective is: certain, complex or uncertain. Then allocate enough time to the issue and design a suitable process to tackle it. A couple of years ago a supermarket chain advised a Government Department how to 'run their meetings more effectively'. One of their key recommendations was that 'no meeting should last longer than an hour'. Assiduously Chairs of meetings made sure that discussion was kept to a minimum, that things moved along, and as the hour approached the decisions were made and announced. It all worked fine until these decisions were tested. Things started to go wrong and issues were found to be compounding. Why was this? Why did the supermarket suggest this approach? The answer lies a) in a misunderstanding of the two different worlds and b) the nature of many of the (operational) meetings that were held in the stores. Most issues *in the store* are by nature *certain*. They pertain to events and actions that are clearly defined and have a readily accessed answer. Therefore, it is reasonable to tell managers to keep discussion and debate to the topic in hand and that they should be able to complete their daily management meeting in under an hour. Not so in a policy world where even the question needs careful definition. This misrepresentation of the two different contexts led to advice that was misguided and ultimately damaging in the context.

I was once asked to coach a project manager who, it was said, could not handle meetings well. In observing him at work, it was apparent that he was trying to resolve all the issues at the 'morning meeting'. This meant that discussion was fractured, tempers frayed and solutions in short supply. All that we had to do was identify the 'certain' issues and deal with them on the spot, at the morning meeting. The 'complex' issues were allocated to a manager to take away and come back with proposals at the weekly meeting where they were discussed in more depth. The 'uncertain' issues were given to a sub group that was tasked with finding the question and asked to bring that to the weekly meeting. His hour-long daily meeting went down to about 40 minutes, the solutions were more effective and the project seemed to handle intractable issues well. Suddenly he was transformed into an excellent project manager! He had not changed but he had distinguished between certainty; complexity and uncertainty and managed them much better.

Levels of Process Awareness
Not all groups are alike – that is an obvious statement! Not all groups are at the same stage of development. Many of you will have come across the Forming; Storming; Norming and Performing model of assessing group development. Another way of defining group progress is in terms of their approach to *uncertainty* and *process*. So having dealt with degrees of uncertainty it is now time to focus on *Levels of Process Awareness*.

The Dysfunctional Group

The Dysfunctional group gives little heed to process. They prefer rigid, well-defined ways of tackling tasks. They actively dislike and distrust *process*, even thinking that it is 'soft' and irrelevant. This leads them to use the same approach to *every* situation. Often the greater the intellect of the managers, the more they believe that every problem can be solved by a 'good debate'. They do not see the need to use models, tools and techniques and actually think this rather beneath them.

Stage 1 – Dys-Functional	**There is strong leadership and the agenda is set. The Group can only manage if there is a rigid procedure which everyone follows.**
Stage 2 - Transitional	**The Group begins to utilise different formats, procedures become more flexible, inter-actions improve and the group begins to take an active interest in process**
Stage 3 - Process Aware	**The Group will recognise uncertainty and adapt the process appropriately. Individuals will take responsibility for the process.**

Conversely managers who have 'come up from the shop floor' often think that by tackling the problem head-on they can resolve it! Both types are dysfunctional, both prefer strong, effective leadership and in many instances this is needed, if only to make the ultimate decision, after the debate and arguing has not resolved the problem. Dysfunctional groups are recognisable by the following characteristics: lack of process; unwillingness to use any aids (such as flip charts, white boards); heavy reliance on PowerPoint presentations; one way conversations and the same people contributing, no matter what the subject. These groups sit around the same table, in the same places and rarely get up or move around. They NEVER break into sub groups (distrusting what the others might be saying or deciding). Inevitably, the chair or leader has most 'power' and uses it. However, success is patchy and the group relies heavily on 'out of meeting' agreements and decisions. If the leader is weak then the group becomes not only dysfunctional but also 'chaotic'. Decisions become haphazard, members become disillusioned and the 'success rate' is very hit and miss.

Transitional Groups

Transitional groups, on the other hand, have learnt that process is valuable. They begin to apply process, recognising its worth. A Transitional group is recognisable as follows: members contribute, if not equally, then in a more balanced way and they can work in sub groups, trusting each other to deliver. Use is made of flip charts, the walls and the space. Use is made of the room, and the (Boardroom) table may even be discarded in favour of more utility ones that can be moved around.

> *I know of one team that made the difficult decision to sell the antique table that had adorned their management room in favour of an 'ordinary' more functional table that could be broken into smaller units!*

One or more members of the team begin to take ownership of the process, using SPOs and this is accepted by the team and valued. Not all will be able to think 'green' but they recognise its value and place in their meetings. The result is that decisions are better, success comes more often, the leader co-ordinates and feels less need to 'lead' and be seen to dominate.

Process Aware Groups

Process Aware Groups are the rarity! They have adopted 'green' thinking and each item is prepared with a process to go with it. Items only make the agenda when there is a process to tackle it. In one company, the regular Health and Safety Meeting was re-designed and the facilitator asked to support the Chair and to design a process for all items that came on the agenda. Nothing was discussed in 'Any Other Business' because this was recognised as a potential pitfall. These groups are recognisable by the following characteristics: the table is only a place to put your files on; the whole room is utilised, in fact, the room is 'selected' based on the tasks being tackled; the walls become workspace and people can be heard offering SPOs at every juncture. There will be a wide variety of models, tools and techniques being used, and some will be invented or adapted to suit a particular situation and need – there are no 'favourite' techniques, only ones that are fit for purpose. The leader has become the facilitator and other members regularly take a green lead. Success is common and uncertainty is not feared, in fact uncertainty is seen as a competitive opportunity to be relished. There is ALWAYS a *process review* at the end of meetings and lessons are learnt and remembered, but not turned into a set of rules, rather they become guiding principles for the future.

Feedback Model
Perhaps the most valuable model that anyone can use, be they the 'Facilitator' or someone seeking to 'facilitate', is the *Feedback Model*. It can be considered a 'model' because of how powerful it is. In Uncertainty there is a need to determine the question, to find the real need. This can be daunting and, yet, it is often discovered by the very act of searching for it – IF and only IF someone uses the Feedback Model. In Chapter Three we will talk about different personality types and their different contribution in teams and meetings. Suffice it to say (unless you want to dive off and read the Chapter before resuming here) that 'extroverts (that is those who 'speak to think') will find themselves, in uncertainty, talking more than they normally do. They will be throwing out comments, walking round the issue, metaphorically, examining it and telling everyone what they are thinking. This effort is wasted unless *someone* takes the trouble to tell them what they are saying!

The Feedback Model provides the means to:
- ensure understanding between people
- develop ideas
- 'climb' out of uncertainty
- 'translate' between specialists

Ensure understanding between people
Partly because of our different personality types and partly because we think we know what someone else has said, there is a strong tendency to misunderstand others. Whilst this would be bad enough in the normal course of events, in a meeting designed to uncover problems, resolve issues, make decisions and find solutions, this kind of misunderstanding can be very damaging. It is particularly significant because, if different people have different interpretations of what is being said, then there is the danger of schisms in understanding and consequently, difficulties in trying to find ways forward. If we base our thinking on a wrong understanding then everything from then on is likely to be a misdirected. An analogy would be that, if a wrong part or raw material got into the production process, then therefore everything going down the production line becomes 'contaminated' – so misunderstanding can contaminate the process of producing effective and sound outcomes.

So what can we do? Commonly what most people actually do if they *think* that there may be misunderstanding or a lack of understanding is either:
- ask a question of the speaker *or*
- the speaker asks everyone if they understood

Both lead to more confusion! Whilst questions themselves are valuable, they can cause more misunderstanding and even conflict if they are based on a misunderstanding in the first place. Imagine someone asking for directions to the railway station and the person being asked knowing that the trains aren't running because of a problem on the line, they still might give directions but the information is irrelevant. Even worse, is asking other people if they understand you. There are three potential responses: silence because no one wants to be the one who admits that they do not understand; everyone nodding as if they do understand to divert attention away from themselves and occasionally some brave soul saying that they did not understand. However, the danger of the first two responses outweighs the advantage of asking people if they have understood. Worse still, everything from then on is built on a false premise that there was complete awareness and understanding of the points being made.

So what can people do? What MUST they do? The answer is to *give feedback* and to *ask for feedback.*

Giving feedback means taking the (small) risk of telling the speaker what you understood them to say. This does not mean feeding back verbatim what they said, rather it is translating it into your own words and reflecting your interpretation of what the speaker meant (see the model below).

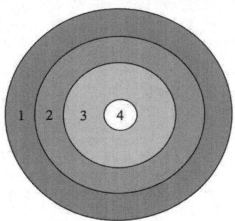

1 - Misunderstanding or misinterpreting what was said.
2 - Missing out some important points or some details
3 - Feeding back accurately and fully what was said
4 - Getting behind the words to the 'hidden' message

There are four potential outcomes of feeding back what you heard being said:

'1' - You will have *completely misunderstood* what the speaker was saying – in which case either you were not listening and, given that you are intending to feedback, this is unlikely. Or, and this is much more likely, what the person said was very difficult to understand or else they themselves did not fully comprehend what they were saying. Strange as it may seem, this happens in uncertainty and extroverts in particular, speak their thoughts as a way of coping with uncertainty. Often in grappling to understand the issues they start to articulate the question. Feeding back helps them and the group to begin to make sense of the problem.

'2' - You have missed *some points* or *not quite grasped all* of what was being said. This often happens when an expert is speaking or there are several thoughts interwoven in the speaker's mind. This can happen with an 'unstructured intuitive' who weaves different concepts together in their mind. Whilst the gist of what is being said can be clear, some parts may have not have made sense or may not have come across clearly.

'3' - You may reflect *accurately* what the person was saying and have grasped the points being made. In which case there is clarity between the speaker and the receiver. Obviously this is the desired position.

'4' - You might be able to feedback *what the person did not say.* This does not mean that you interpret something different! It is not a 'political' mechanism for interpreting something your way. Rather it means that you have 'seen' something that *follows on* from what the speaker has said, or could *rightfully* be inferred (in a positive) sense. This is very powerful and helps groups make sense of uncertainty. If you remember the management team in the leisure park and their deliberations about the pitches (page 21). They would have come to the realisation of the problem and the solution by feeding back and eventually someone giving a '4', by saying something like "So what we are saying is...we do not want to *evict* them, rather we want to *prevent* them from even playing on the pitches".

Therefore, we need to ask the question "Is a '1' or a '2' wrong?" "Is it 'bad' to give a '1' or a '2'"? The answer, of course, is emphatically "No!" Unless the team is dysfunctional, in which case it will be harder to give feedback, the effect of giving feedback is to encourage the speaker to realise that they may have not made clear what they were saying. If the situation is uncertain then they could not help that and any feedback will benefit the group. In other circumstances, when an expert or specialist is speaking, then to know that they have not been fully understood gives them another opportunity to clarify their point. If the opposite happens and everyone sits there dumb and quiet when they ask "Did everyone understand?" then they risk never getting their specialist point across, with the subsequent risk that the group will make poor decisions and they will feel alienated from the group and the outcome.

So, why do groups *not* feed back? Firstly, the reason for this is ignorance of the power of this model. Secondly is the fear that they will be ridiculed for feeding back what is obvious to others and finally, the reason is feeling that you are taking too big a role upon yourself. Each of these reasons belong to dysfunctional groups and one of the key characteristics of a Transitional and Process Aware group is their willingness and ability to give feedback and to work with '1s' and '2s' to build understanding and consensus and meaningful solutions.

So who does the feedback? The answer is someone or anyone! In a Transitional group, 'someone' will hopefully feedback. In a Process Aware group, 'anyone' will take it upon themselves to feedback. In a dysfunctional group 'no one' will risk feeding back and the Facilitator will be left it to do it.

Therefore, what are the mechanics of this simple yet profoundly effective Model, which can be used in any situation to ensure clarity of understanding? Well, the responder uses words like "So if I understand you correctly ...you are saying that...?"

These words and other phrases help lead into asking the person if what *you* are feeding back is what they were saying or meant to say. Invariably, people respond extremely positively to feedback. It makes them feel as though someone was *actually* listening.

> *"So what you're saying is …"*
>
> *"If I understand …"*
>
> *"My understanding is that …"*
>
> *"Can I just check what you're saying…"*
>
> *" I think that you're saying that…"*

It makes them realise whether or not you are making sense. Everyone wants to be understood and make their point effectively. Its use is not confined to meetings, people should be encouraged to use it all the time: in everyday interactions; whenever people are trying to build a common understanding or simply passing on information.

On one occasion, I was invited to review the pay and reward negotiations that had just been completed at a factory. Now this plant was infamous for poor industrial relations and when the announcement came that a settlement had been reached in record time with a massive positive agreement there was interest in how it had been achieved. The manager had learnt the value of the feedback model and had decided to use it in the negotiations. So every time a statement was made by the Union representatives, she would say "So are you saying ...?" or "So if I understand...". This had two immediate and powerful effects, firstly, she was seen to be paying rapt attention because she was able to feedback what the representative said and secondly, and perhaps more importantly, when she did not understand the feedback model elicited a clarification. She also utilised the SPO tool, so that whenever she had a proposal to make she introduced it with her background rationale and finished by outlining the benefits and outcomes. However, she did two other things, which were of real significance. She used 'reverse feedback'. Reverse feedback, is where you encourage the other person to tell you what you have said. Think about it for a moment. You have said something, you are desperate to ensure that you have been understood and yet you cannot feedback to yourself. Therefore, you invite the other person to tell you what they think you have said. The words you use depend on the relationship you have with the other person and whether they know the Feedback Model (which of course helps!). Nevertheless, what you say in so many words is, "So what am I saying...?" Using this reverse feedback in the negotiations ensured that in a 'charged' atmosphere of the negotiating room neither side misunderstood the other. In fact, when I questioned the Union Representative they were full of praise for the manager and her ability and skill in making sure both sides understood each other. By using feedback and reverse feedback it ensured that the discussions were built upon understanding and meant that where there were areas of disagreement they were real and genuine, not the result of some misunderstanding in the heat of the moment. However, she did one other thing. Whenever the Union Representative made a proposal she encouraged them to 'surround' it with an 'S' and a 'O'. So that both sides were clear about the context and the effect of each other's proposals. If the 'S' was ill informed or did not fit with the reality of the situation the other 'side' had an opportunity to challenge it, rather than the proposal. If the 'O' did not stack up then they could challenge that too. The result was that the negotiations went smoothly and were not only well received but completed in a record time for that site!

Exercises

You may find the following exercises useful, especially if you are a Theorist or Pragmatist, to establish the principles and concepts in your mind:

Levels of Process Awareness

What are the characteristics of your team/group? What Level of Process Awareness does this signify?

What actions would help your own team/group to become more Process Aware?

Feedback Model

Have a go at feeding back in any of the following situations:

- a meeting when you know no one else understands (do not be tempted to as a question) *try* and feedback as much as you have understood.
- when arranging some transaction (e.g. getting your car serviced/repaired/booking a complicated flight ticket) – in fact anytime!

What was the result? What impression did it make on others? Did it help the situation?

SPO

Try using a SPO in a range of different situations.

What impact did it have? How did it help? Did people notice?

Degrees of Uncertainty

Look at the next Agenda you receive. Annotate each item as to whether it is: *certain; complex* or *uncertain.* Note how much time has been allocated to each item or if no one has identified a time for each item estimate how much time *you* think it should take. You might even ask other people how long they think it will take.

When you come out of the meeting re-visit your estimates and see if the time you (and others) allocated: a) follows the 2½ and 4½ Rule and if you estimated correctly. Do this several times, until you are able to estimate accurately the time a meeting will last. Of course, if the meeting is badly run, without process, there is no guarantee that, even given extra time the output will be effective!

Examine any project in which you have been involved. Was the time estimate accurate? Do you, on reflection, see certain project milestones that were inaccurate? Were certain activities taken as *certain* when in fact they were *uncertain?* Did this require longer time than was anticipated?

Chapter Two - The Key Roles
- o   Task Leader's role
- o   Facilitator's role

Having laid the groundwork and set in place some of the key concepts of facilitation it is now time to look at key principles, which are based on these concepts. If you accept the concept that there are two elements, ('red' and 'green' thinking) to the production of ideas, problem solving, solution finding and decision making then you are drawn to the conclusion that both are important and both needed if you are to get successful outcomes. It follows, therefore, that there are two related roles.

Task Leader's Role
If, as was said earlier, there is a legitimate role for the facilitator in guarding and focusing on the green process then "Is there a corresponding 'red' role, someone focusing on the objective?" The answer is yes in the following circumstances:

- when the objective is unclear and there is a high degree of *uncertainty* it is helpful to have someone acting in the role of 'Task Leader'. This person's role is not to try to drive out the answer, or bully people into their way of thinking but rather to act as guardian of the task and to help the group focus on the objective as it emerges. This IS a role for a specialist or at least someone who knows something about the issues. This person should be aware of the potential for the group to panic and seek to get into certainty before the real issues have been identified. On the other hand, they should be confident enough to challenge the group if it wanders too far in its search for the objective but without posing their own will on the team members. Again, their key skill and tool will be the use of the Feedback Model. It will help the group clarify where they have reached and what they have discovered.

- when the group is up against tight time scales, it can help to have a Task Leader who focuses the efforts of the group on the key issues and avoids digressions that are not helpful given the time pressure and the need for an output. In this instance, the Task Leader's role is not like the Facilitator, who 'slows' the process down, their role is different, it is 'focus' and direction. It is from the Task Leader that the Facilitator takes their lead and designs process to deliver what the Task Leader wants to achieve. If the group is Process Aware and are skilled at handling process, then this role might well be shared between the individuals and the Task Leader, as they will all be skilled at handling task issues.

The style of the Task Leader is determined in much the same way as in the Situational Leadership Model – see the diagram below:

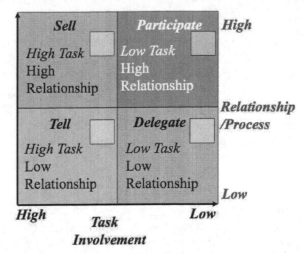

Tell

The Task Leader decides that they have sufficient (task/expertise) knowledge to 'lead' and there is a low requirement for process involvement by the group. The Task Leader decides to operate in the 'Tell' mode. This means that they present the solution to the group and in a sense 'dictate' what will happen. Although this seems to fly in the face of a democratic consensus there are many times when this style is appropriate. If the group has limited expertise/knowledge or the leader decides to carry the responsibility for the decision themselves then the 'Tell' mode is appropriate.

Sell

If the Task Leader believes that although the group has limited expert knowledge, they should be more involved then the 'Sell' mode is more appropriate. The Task Leader suggests the way forward and presents, in effect, a SPO to the group to make their case. This allows more involvement and requires more process activity.

Participative

The Task Leader would be advised to adopt a participative style if the group has the expertise and knowledge. In which case there will again be a need for high levels of Process Involvement and activity to harness the skills and specialist knowledge of the group. The Task Leader will in this instance be operating much more in a coaching and supportive role and helping the group to find the answers. The Task Leaders are still very much involved and will offer their opinion and perceptions but the decision-making will fall much more heavily on the process, rather than the person. Again, we see the need for the Facilitator to provide effective process to guide the task through its various stages.

Delegate
The Task Leader acknowledges that the group has sufficient knowledge, skill and confidence to tackle the task without input from them. The significance of this position is that the Task Leader is transferring responsibility and authority to the group and therefore must by inference, be willing to accept the outcomes and decisions they make. If this is not the case then the Task Leader must *not* delegate the task.

The significance of determining the Task Leader's role is crucial in two key ways:

- the group needs to know what responsibility and authority it has and how it is shared with the Task Leader.

- the Facilitator needs to know the role that the Task Leader is going to play. Are they leading the group? On the other hand, are they only part of the group? The declaration of their role is key in achieving a right relationship between the Facilitator, Task Leader and the group. Democracy and empowerment exist within the bounds of the agreed roles and responsibilities.

Facilitator's Role
Therefore, you begin to see the 'role' of the 'Facilitator'. They are the one who 'guards' the process, who gives heed to the need for process and designs it for the group to use. Therefore, you might well ask, "Why doesn't the group do that for themselves?" The answer lies in a lack of process awareness and their inability to think 'green' and to focus on it when they get embroiled in the heat of the task. Remember that in a factory the process is well defined, well established and monitoring it results in effective production. In a factory, it is the new product development (NPD) that needs attention because it is easy to keep simply producing what is made every day. In effective management meetings the process (green thinking) has to be constantly monitored and updated as the issues change, sometimes minute by minute and certainly each time the group re-visit the situation.

So when is it valuable to have a 'Facilitator'? Well the answer is in the following circumstances:

- when the objective is *uncertain* and people are struggling to even grapple with the issues. Then a dedicated Facilitator can be of value and help keep the process alive by 'doing' most of the 'green' thinking on behalf of the group. Of course, the Facilitator must keep giving Feedback and using SPOs because this will educate the group and build awareness of process – using the most appropriate tools and techniques.

- when the group is *Dysfunctional,* as a process leader, to guide the group to recognise and appreciate the importance and significance of 'green' thinking. Or *Transitional* as a coach to develop their skills. Later in the Chapter, you will see the different styles the facilitator uses in these different circumstances.

- when time is tight and the group feel under pressure to deliver an outcome a Facilitator can help in two ways: focusing on the process and slowing the process down. Whilst the first reason is obvious, when a group is under (time) pressure best practice is in danger of being forgotten but the second is less obvious. 'Slowing the process down', in a sense this is an extension of the first, the Facilitator makes the group 'go through the process' and use the techniques and tools, rather than take shortcuts. Have you ever tried to leave for an important appointment and found yourself doing things twice, even three times? You transfer the phones and muck up the sequence of numbers. You try and close your computer and fail to log off properly. You leave your keys lying somewhere and have to hunt for them. That is because your normal routine (process) is rushed in your desire to move quickly. It is the same when a group is under a time pressure, they forego best practice and try to do things more quickly and end up re-doing them because they do not do them properly. The Facilitator gets the group to slow down and work carefully and to follow through with the tools and techniques.

So when can a group facilitate themselves? Well the answer is in some ways the opposite of the previous reasons:

- the group has matured, is *Transitional* and has made significant head way in adopting 'green' thinking. There have to be people in the group who 'think green' and who can step out of the task when required to reflect on the process and make process suggestions.

- the task is *certain or complex* and the group know that they can handle it with tools and techniques that they are familiar with (though not just by using people's 'favourite' ones).

A Process Aware group may ask a facilitator to watch to see how it is operating, simply to see if it is falling into any bad habits and to audit its processes. Sometimes a group can become blasé and then when it has to tackle an *uncertain* task, it falters and loses confidence.

Subject matter expert or not?
A logical question which people comes into people's minds at about this time is whether a Facilitator needs to have subject matter expertise if they are to be effective. The question should not be confused with whether people are acting as facilitators as well as being the subject expert. Trainers for example are both subject experts *and* facilitate the course or workshop. However, the trainer has developed (in a similar way to a factory manager) an established process for managing the course content.

It is my contention, after numerous years 'facilitating' a wide variety of situations and covering an equally wide range of issues and topics that the Facilitator does *not* need any specialist knowledge of the subject matter. In fact it can be a disadvantage in at least two ways: first the Facilitator can become distracted by the topic and drift into 'red' thinking; secondly the group may begin to doubt the Facilitator's integrity if the going gets tough, if they suspect that the Facilitator might have a (task) vested interest.

So an equally valid question is: "How does the Facilitator know what to do if they *do not* have specialist knowledge?" The answer lies in the process. A good Facilitator keeps in touch with the topic by giving Feedback. This is not for personal benefit – it should always be done to benefit the group but it does have the effect of keeping the Facilitator conscious of the issues at hand. The facilitator should use, as much as possible, analogies in their feedback. In this way, they test their understanding *outside* the confines of the specialist discussion.

Let me give an example to illustrate my point. I was once asked to facilitate a National Health Service Trust in setting its "Action Plan for Sickle Cell and Thalassaemia". Now to my disgrace I had not heard of either of these medical conditions, so on the face of it I was the last person you would expect to be facilitating the event of 65 people. They represented sufferers of the condition; charities; health workers; managers (of the money) and emergency services. However, as the person leading the event described her objectives for the event to me I started to get a sense of an analogy in my mind. As I was thinking about this and building on it in my thoughts, I kept giving her feedback on what she was saying, avoiding the big words (!) and telling her what I was hearing her say. This had two effects a) she knew I was listening b) it clarified some of her thoughts. I then felt confident enough to give my SPO. I compared the Action Plan with the lifecycle of a car (having first said that this in no way reflected the seriousness of the condition). I suggested that when a new car comes off the production line it is inspected and any problems noticed and recorded. I suggested that as soon as a baby is born, being effective in 'spotting' tell tale signs would help future treatment, "Yes...yes," she said. Then when a car reaches one year it is given a 'service' and sufferers should likewise be able to get regular 'inspections' to see how they are progressing, "Yes....yes. We need regular follow-ups, not just leaving people to come in for help when they are acute". Encouraged by her response I suggested that if a car gets damaged it needs specialist attention from the 'rescue services' (par-medics and ambulance) and specialist care to be repaired. You go to someone who has a good reputation for the kind of specialist repair you need, "Exactly...all the services need to know what to do and we need to have guidance for them so they know how to handle acute/chronic cases...". So maybe, I ventured, we could have a chart on the wall and annotate along the 'life-cycle' what: standards (a word she had used); guidance and activities would be appropriate at each point. "Excellent...very good...yes we could do that..." and at that point we both started putting together the 'process' for getting all 65 people involved. The result was that people voted the event as an excellent use of their time and believed that the outcomes would be very useful. I have a slightly better understanding of Sickle Cell/Thalassaemia but I am not and do not want to become an expert in this subject. I want to develop and hone my skills in creating, designing and deploying models, tools and techniques.

In Chapter Five we look in detail at how the Facilitator contracts with the group and how that contract reflects the style they adopt in the meeting/workshop. However, we need first to understand the *nature* of that role compared to other roles, which managers and groups encounter, namely: trainers and consultants.

Both the consultant and the trainer have *implicit* contracts. They are the 'experts' and people look to them for direction and guidance. The consultant is seen to have technical competence and therefore 'leads', the trainer is also seen to have technical or behavioural skills to impart and as well defines the *process* of learning. So where does that leave the facilitator? They are not task experts and as such cannot give 'technical' advice. They forsake any specialist knowledge they have and instead help groups explore change. Their natural environment is *uncertainty* and their expertise is *process.* When a number of managers were being trained in facilitation skills, they were asked to identify the nature of the facilitator's role. They defined it as 'living in uncertainty' but also having 'expertise and specialist knowledge'. When asked why they saw it like that they responded by saying that, in the same way as a consultant had technical knowledge, the facilitator had 'process knowledge' and was therefore an expert in this field.

THE NATURE OF THE FACILITATOR'S ROLE

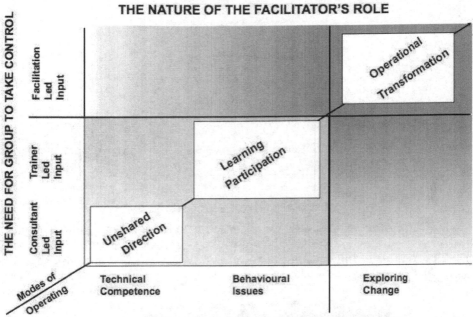

It is therefore important to look at the characteristics of the different roles, the consultant, trainer and facilitator. The consultant is a Task expert; they present solutions and answers; they live in their (past) experience; use that experience for the client's benefit and they are specialist centred. The trainer is: task and knowledge experienced; participative in activity; lives in the known; demonstrates certainty for the delegates benefit and is specialist/trainer focused. The facilitator on the other hand is: a non-task expert; instead they are a process expert; they live and model uncertainty for the client; they model change; they should be risk takers in terms of process; a catalyst and they should be ego-less, expecting the praise for success to rebound back on the group.

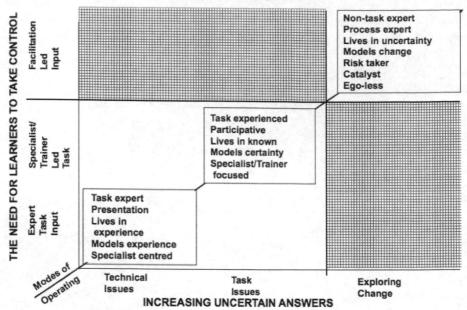

THE CHARACTERISTICS OF THE (CHANGING) ROLE

How, then, does a facilitator work in the process realm with a group? How do they model their role to mirror the group's activities? They need to take account of three dimensions: the nature of the Task; the Maturity of the group and the Time allocated to the event.

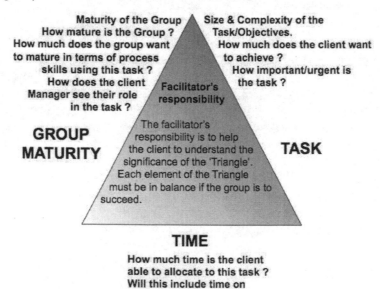

They have to consider all three of these dimensions and bring them into balance. They need to be cognisant of the likelihood of *uncertainty* and its potential to challenge the group's ability to manage it. They need to be aware of the group's level of process awareness and therefore their ability to handle and work with process and to be conscious of time, which can run away in uncertainty. This triune role can best be explained by an illustration. In Diagram 1 the group faces different degrees of uncertainty during their time together (which could be an hour a day or in fact any length of time). The arrows mark the significant changes taking place (in the *Degree of Uncertainty*). In Diagram 2 you can see how the level of process awareness of the group fluctuates in response to the degree of uncertainty as shown in Diagram 3. The arrow highlights how the group *appears* to becoming more *Transitional*, when in fact, it is the reduction in the *Degree of Uncertainty* which has (falsely) led to an apparent increase in maturity.

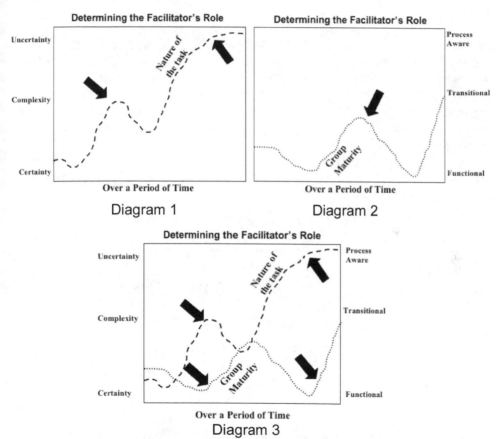

Diagram 1   Diagram 2

Diagram 3

This phenomenon of a group, which appears to be effective and successful, demonstrates signs of immaturity or of being less effective. This is a direct consequence of *uncertainty*. Take for example the situation in the pits of a Formula One racing car team or an Indy Car pit team. They are well trained and well versed in their individual roles and function together as a 'well oiled' team. However, on occasions when a different type of wheel change is ordered at the last moment or a car all of a sudden arrives in the pits and requires a different configuration, the team can sometimes lose valuable milliseconds, which are crucial in getting the car out ahead of the opposition. The same is true in management meetings/workshops. A team/group that performs well in the normal course of their roles suddenly appears to be ill disciplined, agitated and ill at ease when faced with uncertainty. This has the effect of making the team look less competent than they are. It sometimes results in an in-experienced facilitator examining the group dynamics when in fact the problem is the *nature of the task.* A good facilitator takes account of this fluctuation and this different behaviour and modifies their style and role accordingly to compensate for the loss of maturity (in process terms).

In Diagram 4 we see the complimentary style of the facilitator taking more of a process lead as the *nature of the task* becomes more *uncertain* and the *group's (process) maturity* 'dips'. The facilitator takes more of a lead in process terms. This is not meant to last and as soon as the facilitator can 'back-off' they should do so BUT not whilst the task remains uncertain and the group is struggling. The notion that the facilitator sits at the back and watches the group is false. The facilitator needs to lead if necessary. On the other hand, the notion that the facilitator should be at the front all and every time misrepresents the nature of the role.

Determining the Facilitator's Role

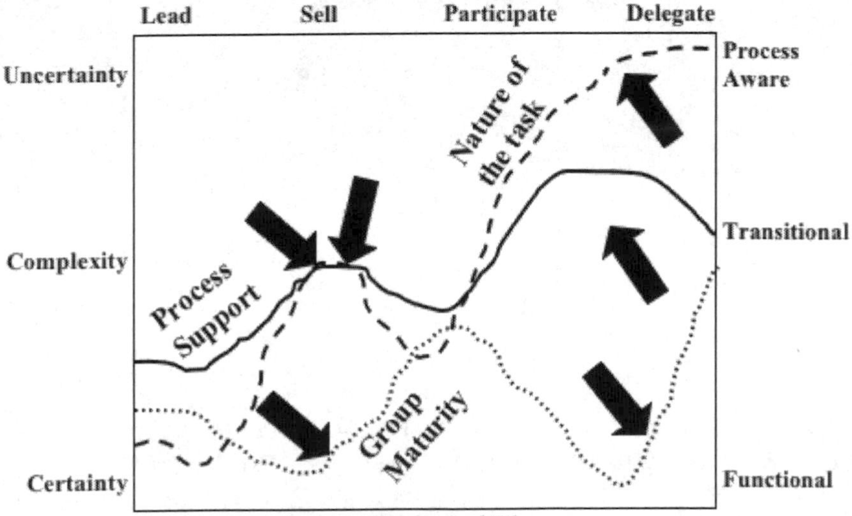

Over a Period of Time

Diagram 4

The Art, Science and Skill of Facilitation

Therefore, the Facilitator's role alters depending on:
-   the nature of the task
-   the maturity of the group
-   the time pressures which might require the facilitator to take more of a process lead to allow the group to focus on the task

In the United Kingdom the emergency services are reached by dialling '999'. In facilitation terms a '9 x 9 x 9' is when the nature of the Task is *uncertain,* the group's *Level of Process Awareness* is dysfunctional and the time available is very limited. A '999' requires an experienced and confident Facilitator who understands: the nature of their role; the pressure on the group because of the situation and who can take (process) risks to help the group.

In Chapter 5 we will see how this translates into a 'contract' with the group and how the Facilitator knows how to set that contract to best serve the group's needs.

Chapter Three - Knowing Myself …Understanding Others
- o Myers Briggs Type Indicator®
- o Understanding the different Types
- o Different Types …different techniques

Good facilitators know their own personality 'type', the implications of that  for themselves and how they (re)act. Furthermore, they can recognise others' 'types' and know how to match them with models, tools and techniques to suit them. The misnomer is that members of a group should *all* be doing the same thing and using the same technique *at the same time.* However, the man in the photo below was working in a group of 24 senior managers building a 'process map' as part of an examination of a bigger objective. Whilst others were working together in threes and fours he preferred to work alone, sitting on the floor.

Myers Briggs Type Indicator® (MBTI)[1]
The MBTI offers a personality 'typing' tool, which helps a facilitator understand people, and the way that they are likely to work. It comprises: four dimensions (see Table below); sixteen 'types' made up of different combinations of the dimensions (e.g. ISTJ, ENFP) and reflects the different work styles and approach which encompass most people. Each 'Type' has its own characteristics, which reflect such aspects as: relationship to people and interaction; handling information; making decisions and way of working.

Type	
Extrovert	**I**ntrovert
Sensing	i**N**tuitive
Thinking	**F**eeling
Judgemental (Structured)	**P**erceptive (Unstructured)

Table

---

[1] The Myers Briggs Type Indicator® and MBTI are registered trademarks of Consulting Psychologists Press, Inc

Most people are on one side of the 'line' or the other and the degree to which a person is along that line will dictate how strongly they reflect that dimension (see the diagram below).

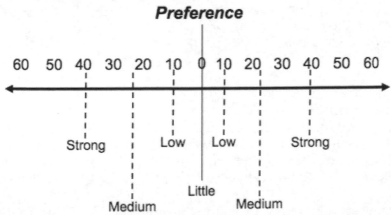

Some people are on the border between the two and in that case, they have characteristics of both dimensions. Others show degrees of the 'Type' ranging from 'Low' to 'Strong'. The characteristics of the four dimensions are as follows:

Extroverts

Extroverts 'speak to think'. They enjoy conversation as a means of exploring and examining what they are thinking. They prefer to 'bounce' ideas around, no matter how unformed the idea is. They enjoy interaction because they see people as a resource to enable them to think. To them thoughts are like sonar. The signal (their thought) goes out, hopefully to a sympathetic listener and the response comes back and triggers another thought (as the cartoon shows). This process can go on for any length of time and Extroverts are known to change their minds several times during a conversation. The implication of this is that they need someone to 'bounce' back their thoughts and to reflect back what they are saying. Left alone they actually find it more difficult to think.

Introverts

Introverts 'think to speak'. They enjoy contemplation as a means of exploring and examining what they want to say. They prefer to mull ideas over, no matter how well formed they are. They enjoy solitude (in their thinking) because they have the opportunity to develop their ideas and thoughts uninterrupted. In this way they can formulate their thoughts and 'package' them ready for display. This process of contemplation and 'mulling' can go on for any length of time and if any new thought is planted in their mind it causes a 'recycling' and reformulation of the ideas. In the company of talkative people demanding attention they find it more difficult to think clearly.

The Extrovert will 'speak to think'. The implication of this is that the Extrovert is 'driven' to speak in order to make sense of what they are thinking. They 'download' ideas, thoughts, whatever is in their mind as a means of 'testing their thinking'. Meanwhile the Introvert 'thinks to speak' and is content to think awhile, perchance to (eventually) speak once they have got their thoughts sorted. The result of this 'mismatch' is that Extroverts value discussion and conversation and Introverts value silence and time for reflection.

Sensing

Sensing 'types' like data. They absorb information and relish being able to find out about things. Sensing types prefer to build their case on established facts and dislike having to make assumptions. They use all five senses in order to gain understanding and insights into what is happening. Sensing types like the here and now and use historical information/statistics/data to build a picture of the future.

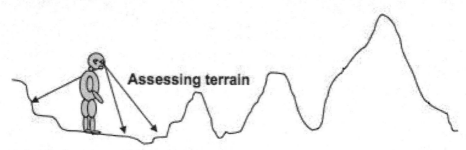

Assessing terrain

Intuitive

Intuitive 'types' like hypothesis. They make intuitive 'leaps' and enjoy creating new patterns from what they know. They use their 'sixth' sense in order to gain understanding and an insight into what is happening.

Intuitive types like the future possibilities and use their imagination to build a picture of the future.

Imagining what lies over the hill

The Senser likes facts and information. The Intuitive likes patterns and models. The Senser starts from *what is.* The Intuitive starts from *what might be.* They take a different stance on evidence. Past events are important to the Senser the future possibilities are important to the Intuitive.

Thinking

Thinking types look at situations in a logical, dispassionate way. They prefer to make assessment by looking coolly at the facts as they are

  presented. They make their decisions objectively based on the information they have. They tend to appear somewhat 'detached' and separate as if they were viewing things as a bystander. To say that they 'think' things is a truism. To them everything can be subjected to logical reasoning. Thinkers base their decisions on 'principles' which fit the time and situation.

Feeling

Feeling types look at situations in a personal almost passionate way. They prefer to make assessment by looking at the facts as they are

presented from a personal perspective. They make their decisions based on 'rights' and 'wrongs' of the situation. They tend to appear somewhat 'involved' viewing things as an insider. To say that they 'feel' things is a truism. To them everything must be subjected to personal viewpoint. Feelers base their decisions on 'values' which are deeply felt.

Feelers and Thinkers make their decisions from different perspectives. Feelers like to be involved. Thinkers are dispassionate. Feelers want the best for everyone. Thinkers want the best from the situation.

Judgemental (Structured)
Judgemental is an unhelpful word in understanding this type. Judgementals are at their core structured, organised, planners. They like

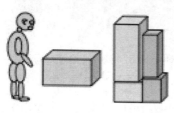

to organise themselves and the situation around them. Judgementals prefer things to be in order and to have a place. They like to know what is going to happen and to feel in control of the situation. Judgementals never leave things to the last minute preferring to tie things down and have them neatly put in place. Judgementals never leave anything to chance, they like to take control and ensure that everything has been considered.

Perceptive (Unstructured)
Perceptive is an unhelpful word in understanding this type. Perceptives are at their core unstructured, unorganised, and dislike planning. They like to keep things and the situation around them more flexible. Perceptives prefer things to be adaptable and to have no set routine. They like to feel that anything could happen. They do not like to be constrained by their circumstances. Perceptives leave things to the last minute preferring to allow things to evolve and 'grow'. Perceptives like

leaving things to chance; they dislike control and like to think that if they leave things a little bit longer new things might enter the equation for the good.

Perceptives like flexibility and end up leaving things to the last minute. Judgementals like order and dislike leaving things, preferring to get them done and settled. Perspectives prefer spontaneity and adapting as they go. Judgementals prefer structure and getting things organised ahead of schedule.

Understanding the Different Types
The different dimensions make for sixteen different Types each one with a different set of characteristics. However, for the facilitator *each* dimension provides the key to understanding the differences and to being able to manage the group dynamics. Being aware of someone who is talking a lot and recognising an Extrovert and understanding their need to

explore their thinking will ensure that you are sympathetic to that person. Noticing someone who is quiet and not taking part in a discussion and recognising that they may well be an Introvert will ensure that you do not try and make them take part but leave them to think!

Hearing someone wanting more information and demanding more facts will alert you to the possibility of a Sensing (person). Hearing someone making hypothetical remarks and making 'leaps' of imagination will cause you to wonder if they are an Intuitive (person). Neither is wrong in their need and both may find the other frustrating.

When it comes to decision time you may notice arguments put forward dispassionately and others arguing 'from the heart'. There may be loud voices and keen debate. There may be a sense of disunity and of people at odds with each other. The Feeler and Thinker will not hold back in building their case.

Someone, you sense, wants to see *how* this is all going to work. Someone else is happy that the group explore the issues and hold off any decisions. One person appears unhappy with the way the task is being tackled, another seems quite happy. At another moment someone asks, "Where is this taking us?" and another counters with "Can't you just wait and see?" Judgementals and Perceptives will hold a different viewpoint about the way things are going.

Is there any hope for the Facilitator? Yes, if firstly, they recognise the different Types and they do NOT take it personally. Secondly, they should NOT see disagreement and disharmony as a break down of the team's morale. Thirdly, they should recognise that each type has different needs: to talk – to be silent; to look at facts – to think the impossible; to make logical decisions – to think of the people; to be ordered and structured – to be adaptable and see what happens.

Different types…Different techniques
So what can the Facilitator do faced with these diametrically opposed poles? They can design the process and format to suit ALL Types! Impossible you may think. No! If you know your tools and techniques well enough you can structure the design of the process to *meet the needs of the different types.* For example, *Allegory – A Day at the Zoo* will suit ENFPs much better then ISTJs. Relative Importance Grid will suit ISTJs much better than ENFPs. Using 'Dots' will work in reverse. If you have never tried it, try using *Dots and* Relative Importance Grid at the same time and inviting people to choose which one they want to use. The results will be very similar; however, the different types will be much

more positive using the technique, which suits their personality Type. Intuitives like to use Post Its™ and put them into themes and patterns and make 'models' of the information. Sensers like to structure the information hierarchically and sequentially. Both will come to a similar conclusion but in different ways. Sometimes, because the task demands it you will need to press upon a group the need to use a particular tool/model such as *Force Field Analysis.* This suits E/I STJs much more than other types. You will need to construct an SPO to ensure that you get buy-in and that you convince people to apply themselves. Remember, not everyone has to *do* the technique as long as they do not opt out or sabotage the process. The 'bystanders' can play an important role, they can, instead, watch and draw conclusions and give feedback on what they see emerging.

One tool fits all should NOT be in a facilitator thinking. The facilitator should instead be watching the group, looking for signs of distress and thinking of alternatives tools/techniques that they could offer.

Everyone having to do the same thing, should NOT be in the facilitator's thinking. The Facilitator should instead be thinking how they could use different tools and techniques to achieve the same objective.

Chapter 5 looks at how the facilitator takes any emotional disturbance as a signal to examine the team role Types and to assess whether they need to change the process or format.

Understanding personality, 'Types' can be a great aid to the facilitator. Whatever model you use, become an expert in it. Learn to recognise the different types and understand how they react in different situations and know which tools and techniques suit the different Types. Take any emotion as a signal that the person is out of their comfort zone and think about how you can change the process to make it work for them. After all your job is to help the group to deliver outputs. Only if the group has asked you to stretch them, and in my experience, most groups use a 'facilitator' to get results, not experiment, should you knowingly take people out of their comfort zone.

Chapter Four - Preparing for an Event/Workshop
- o Meeting the 'client'
- o Hearing the 'real' need
- o Planning the Agenda/Change Format
- o Selecting and Organising the Venue

Meeting the 'client'
There could be several meetings with the client depending on whether the Facilitator and the client have already worked together or are meeting for the first time.

First Meeting
Often the first meeting can be exploratory. The client may even be wondering if facilitation is 'right for them'. What does the Facilitator say on these occasions? How do they promote their 'service'? Whilst you are not a salesperson, you do have to explain the added value of facilitation (over other approaches) and explain what you will do. The following is intended as a guide, not a script to be followed religiously:

- you can help the client and the group to *achieve their objectives* that is what you are there for. Some Facilitators see themselves as coaches to the group. However, essentially a Facilitator is there to achieve *outcomes*, not to manage 'group dynamics'. Yes, you may handle some inter-personal interactions. Yes, you will 'manage' the group but you will do this by *process* not intervening at a personal level. Clients are wary of facilitators who come on the pretext of helping the group to achieve some outcome and then spend their time delving into the group's internal relationships. This may sound harsh but facilitation, if it is about anything, is about reaching some conclusion, achieving some outcome. If you have to deal with some inter-personal issues in doing so, so be it, but you only do this to achieve the outcome. In Chapter 6 you will see how this is set up and in Chapter 7 how it is manifested.

- you provide *process input*
  Your expertise lies in *process* and it is one of the hardest things to explain until you have seen a good Facilitator in action. If the group is dysfunctional, the last thing people can imagine is *process* interventions. It will be alien to them and if they have seen poor facilitation and, sadly there is a lot of it about, they will be prejudice against *process.* You have to develop a 'language' using some examples and an explanation of *what* process is. Do NOT underestimate the importance of this discussion. However,

the worst thing you can do is to start sharing your own experiences and your past 'successes'. They will mean NOTHING to the client, unless they happen to be a Theorist learner and, even then, if the examples do not relate to their situation it is likely to miss the target. So what should you do?

- Ask the client what they are *hoping to achieve*
  The best way to explain your skills and what you can offer is to relate it *directly* to the situation that the client is facing. Ask the client to tell you what they want to achieve. Then sit back (not too relaxed) and LISTEN! Remember 'listening' means, in fact, giving feedback. So keep feeding back to the client what you hear being said. You will be amazed at how the relationship grows and flourishes, almost immediately. People rarely have others do them the honour of listening AND demonstrating that they have heard what they said. You will learn a great deal about the issues and the objective(s) and you should add value straight away as your feedback causes the client to (re)think what they were planning. Often what they want will be 'uncertain' and your feedback will cause them to re-frame their ideas. You will automatically begin to break the objective down in to tasks and to begin to order them to create a sequence of tasks and activities. Feeding this back to the client should convince them of your value. As you and the client work your way through the '1s' and '2s' to reach a common understanding you should begin to earn the respect of the client.

> *I remember being phoned by a potential client who had come across us on the internet. It was as speculative as that! As he began to share the situation he faced I fed back what I heard him saying. The more I fed back the more '3s' (see the Feedback Model) I got and the more comfortable he got. Two weeks later, I received a call and was invited me to facilitate his quarterly meetings. When I asked him why he had selected me he replied that "You understood what I wanted better than anyone else I asked and you seemed to know what I was trying to change and how I wanted to make this meeting different." This was because I am meticulous in giving Feedback and ensuring understanding of the need! I had not in the conversation given any examples of my experience, though I subsequently sent a PowerPoint slide presentation with words and photos describing our philosophy and client base.*

- Offer the client *SPOs*
  The other benefit of listening and feeding back is that you should begin to 'hear' the process words (see Chapter Seven). There comes a time when you should have heard enough to begin to see what Models, Tools and Techniques you could use to achieve outcomes for each task and activity. This is where you really earn respect. You can summarise the situation, the need, and the tasks and then link them to *process.* Take your time explaining *each* model, tool and technique. Describe how it works and how you propose using it and then explain what the outcome will be. Show this visually as well as in words. Draw a matrix linking the tasks and the process. Draw diagrams to explain the techniques (e.g. the Four Box Model).

Objective Tasks and *Activities*	Process Models, *Tools & Techniques*

A colleague and I did this with a potential client. He was very dubious about 'facilitation' having previously had a bad experience. He only agreed to talk to us because he valued the opinion of one of his team (who had previously worked with us). When we gave our SPO he was amazed and said "Yes..yes..that's what I want..!" We asked him what his previous facilitators had done, and as much I could understand, they were trainers who had, in effect, taken the brief and constructed some training around the objective! It was NOT facilitation as I understood it and certainly not as he wanted it. We went on to facilitate the project review of the largest outsourcing contract of buildings that the military had undertaken.

- you do NOT get involved in the task
  You need to explain that you are *not* a task expert and will not get involved in the task. This often comes as a relief to clients who

may have bad experiences of consultants offering to facilitate only as a means of putting their specialist viewpoint forward. Explain that whilst you will help people to uncover the issues you will not have opinions or take positions.

> *I often tell people that I know nothing about their business and that I am not interested! Before they have chance to get upset I reiterate that I am there to provide process support NOT business expertise!*

- you will 'slow' the event down
  This seems an odd thing to say. However, the reality is that your presence will *slow* the meeting/event/workshop down (and therefore you need to inform your client early on). Your *process* interventions will have the effect of reviewing the 'red' discussions. You will be feeding back and checking understanding, something that may be alien to the group. Overall, with the time required to use the process models, tools and techniques it will seem longer.

- the outputs WILL be better that they have had before
  In all of this you can assure the client that the outcome will be better!

- you are not a consultant or a trainer
  Ensure that the client is clear about the difference between a consultant, a trainer and a facilitator. Once you have explained the key differences in the roles (see Chapter Two) use 'reverse feedback' to check that they really have grasped the difference.

- you may want to say that you do not do fun !
  > *I like to differentiate myself from 'teambuilding' where the emphasis is on 'bonding' and developing effective interactions. I will sometimes say "We don't DO fun!" This is to highlight that we are there to ensure an outcome and that we tend only to use models, tools and techniques which match the task. Therefore, we do not use 'icebreakers' as a general rule. However, we are quick to say that people WILL enjoy it and will go away feeling and thinking that they have spent a useful time together. Strangely, these times often prove to be good for teambuilding because they bond people around common issues and agreed action plans.*

Hearing the 'real' need

This is a continuation of the principles of the first meeting. You should be listening and feeding back as often as you can. Be bold and cut into the conversation if the client insists on telling you everything. They have a tendency to feel that you need to know the whole history of the organisation! You can foreshorten this by the judicious use of feedback, "So what you're saying is that..." "If I understand you correctly.....". This has the effect of demonstrating that you understand. The *additional* benefit of this is that you begin to uncover the *real* need. If you use models such as the Process Iceberg; SCA; Linking; Five Questions and even Is and Is Not then you begin to discover the *real* issues underlying the need for the group to meet. Use Post Its™ to capture what the client is saying (use square ones and smaller ones, write on them and lay them out on an A4 pad). Position the Post Its™ in the 'pattern' of what is being said. Change colours to reflect the different *themes* and sizes to highlight the subsiduarity of the issues. Very soon the client will join in and say something like "No that should be mauve like that issue" and "Yes, there both sub issues but still important within the context of the main objective". Even take dots along (to allocate to each option/issue) or a Relative Importance Grid[2] and help the client to highlight the key issues and main points. This will all add value and is a real and 'live' demonstration of facilitation – for that is what you are doing – identifying the issues and formulating the hierarchy and sequence of tasks and activities. This should be an exciting time for you and the client and it should begin to build an effective working relationship.

Warning note!
Do not be tempted to ask about people and certainly avoid a character description/assassination of members of the group.

> *I once, when I was very inexperienced allowed a client to give me a break down on the whole team and he made sure I took notes. There was one individual that he was obviously 'gunning for'. You will no doubt have guessed the impact of this. In the meeting, I could not help but see everything this person did with a tainted perspective. It made facilitating very difficult and the manager expected me to annihilate this person. Knowing too much about people causes you to become biased and so affects your judgement.*

---

[2] Facilitation – A Handbook of Models, Tools and Techniques for Effective Group Work by the same author - ISBN 978 0 9556435 1 4 p.142

On another occasion a client, let slip to me and my colleagues that they hoped to 'get her to leave'. In the subsequent Industrial Tribunal, we were called as witnesses and asked what we knew about the organisation's plans for her role! Not a nice position to be in! I would rather know nothing about people and as general rule I avoid knowing who is who and who is more senior than another, restricting myself to such things as their job function. This 'rule' has served me well and, apart from a few "Did you know who he/she was!" – as a senior civil servant/Director or Junior Minister left the room, I have found that relying on my ability to assess people's personality type, team role, learning style and their process skills has served me much better and I am seen as adopting a neutral position.

Planning the Agenda Format

So, now we come to the planning. You can liken facilitating an event to writing a piece of choreography for a complicated play or musical. *Process* should be:

- *elegant* – it should 'look' good; it should work well in the situation and, although it may be hard, it should feel worth doing
- *fit for purpose* – this is similar to the above but it is about using the 'right' model, tool or technique for the task. Not being too big and clumsy and not too frail and ineffective.
- *appropriate for the group* – some tools need to be used by expert artisans. Some tools require additional skill and experience to use them. The same is true in facilitating process – some models, tools and techniques are just too hard for some groups to use and although you know that they would do the job the group may not have the process experience to use it. Better to use two tools or a different model than have the group lose confidence in its own ability.

All this reinforces the fact that as a facilitator you need to learn the tools of your trade and be extremely familiar with them. You may on occasions, have to use tools that are fresh to you *IF* they are the right ones for the group. The first time I used Storytelling I had only recently learnt how it do it and had had limited experience. However, an occasion came up where I knew it was the most appropriate tool. The group did not like writing, were not good at spelling and were nervous of embarrassing themselves. Therefore, I did the SPO and the group jumped at the chance to use it. It was a great success and as well as encouraging the group and achieving a positive outcome, it extended my range of models, tools and techniques.

Diagram 1 below shows the *Agenda Format* which is used to translate the (red) objective into (green) process. The Task Leader (see Chapter 2) should invite everyone who has an Item for the Agenda or is involved in planning the workshop/event to provide a short description of their Item or the Objective(s). The Objective(s) should begin with the word *'To....'*. There should be no *'and'...* otherwise this suggests that there is another objective *or* that the statement is not the highest-level objective. If the person cannot identify an objective then this is an indication that the issue is *uncertain.* In this situation accept the description and explore the objective in the meeting/event.

Objectives	Tasks	Degree of Uncertainty
The objectives - that is what is the purpose of the meeting. This will in turn cause them to realise the degree of uncertainty raised by the objective	The sub - tasks ensure that all aspects of the objective get explored. The degree of uncertainty will determine the degree to which the objective is broken down into sub - tasks	The level of uncertainty can then be defined and this will help people to recognise how difficult the task is going to be

Diagram 1

The Task Leader and/or the Facilitator then work through each objective identifying the Tasks/Activities, which will need to take place in order to achieve the Objectives. This should go into as much depth as possible. Avoid the mistake of leaving the Objective at too high a level – it needs to be broken down into the Task steps that will help achieve the required outcome. Usually this will be a joint responsibility. If, however, this approach is very new to a group (e.g. dysfunctional group) then the Facilitator might take more of a lead in identifying the tasks and their sequence. Ideally, though the Facilitator will do this *with* the Task Leader, or if the Task Leader is Transitional/Process Aware they may wish to do it themselves.

Once the tasks are in a logical order, each one (as well as the overall objective) is defined as:
- *Certain* (the question is known and the answer is easily identified)
- *Complex* (the question is known and there will be a number of

potential solutions/answers)

- *Uncertain* (even the question is unclear and will need defining before solutions can be explored).

Note: Although an Objective may be, for example, *uncertain*, an individual task/activity may be *complex.* Remember to leave 4½ times the imagined time to deal with *Uncertainty*!

The first three columns of the Agenda Format (see Diagram 1) are then completed and can be sent back to the originator(s) who are asked:

- if it makes sense?
- will the achieve the Objective(s)?
- will the Item and the Actions generate emotion or will it be neutral?

Once the Tasks/Activities and the level of uncertainty has been defined the Facilitator can determine the process and format (see Diagram 2). The Facilitator should then select the most appropriate approach to tackle the tasks and choose the models, tools and techniques which will:

- be effective in handling the tasks
- suit the group's level of maturity
- fit with the time available

Objectives	Tasks	Degree of Uncertainty	Process/ Format	Time	Preparation
The objectives - that is what is the purpose of the meeting. This will in turn cause them to realise the degree of uncertainty raised by the objective	The sub - tasks ensure that all aspects of the objective get explored. The degree of uncertainty will determine the degree to which the objective is broken down into sub - tasks	The level of uncertainty can then be defined and this will help people to recognise how difficult the task is going to be	Each sub - task may require a different format. The format chosen will depend on: the number of Participants, the level of process awareness of the group, the degree of uncertainty and the time available.	The time needed for each Stage in the Process so that there is an accurate picture of the total time needed.	Finally there may be a need and a benefit that can be gained by undertaking some preparation. This should be identified and individuals tasked with doing it.

Diagram 2

It is vital that the Task Leader feels comfortable with the models, tools and techniques that the Facilitator is proposing. Much of this discussion will take place in their meeting (be that face to face or over the telephone). However, the Facilitator will reflect on the objective and tasks and may well think of different process options. The design of the Process and choices of Format may therefore take several iterations and discussions between the Task Leader and the Facilitator.

Once the process and the format have been designed, the Facilitator will be able to determine the length of each task and therefore the time the objective will take to complete and be able to agree with the Task Leader the time required. If there is a problem with time, the Task Leader and the Facilitator should decide how many and which objectives should stay on the Agenda based on such parameters as urgency and significance (they might even use a Four Box Model: Urgent vs Significance to decide this). The worst scenario and one to be avoided at all costs is the Task Leader deciding to go ahead even if the time is inadequate. The whole point of an Agenda Format is to identify the time requirements accurately and to ensure that the process will deliver the outcomes required. The Facilitator should therefore use all their powers of persuasion to ensure that the tasks are not squeezed and the process short-circuited to fit the time.

I remember once having to facilitate a workshop for a Minister of State, her Junior Ministers and their senior Civil Servants. The Private Secretary gave us (a co-Facilitator and I) the brief and the objectives and together we designed the process to achieve the required outcomes. It became obvious that there was insufficient time to achieve all the objectives. We had taken the precaution of asking for a meeting with the Government Minister and we presented on flip charts the Agenda Format showing each objective and its matching process. As we took her through it she acknowledged that the tasks were valid and that the process would suit the need. She saw the time allocation and acknowledged that if each objective was to be treated with the seriousness that it deserved, then something had to give. She suggested the day begin earlier, that she and her ministers stay longer and that we only tackle objectives one, three and five. It was the meticulous planning, enabled by the Agenda Format, which convinced her and ensured that we had a good workshop.

Finally, the Task Leader and the Facilitator should determine the Preparation that will be required, set that in place, and decide who should carry out it out. Often this preparation uses some of the 4½ time, which is needed in uncertainty.

One year when were facilitating a three day strategic networking event for managers across Europe we asked them to interview three customers each (prior to the Conference) using a template we designed and to bring the data on Post Its™. This saved many hours and in effect ensured that the event was a success.

Finally, the Agenda is issued to the participants. See an example *Agenda Format* at Appendix 4.

Selecting and Organising the Venue

The Agenda Format will determine the nature of the venue and the layout. The venue and the layout are integral to the effective use of process. On the other hand, an excellent Agenda Format can be ruined by lack of attention to the venue and the layout. It is then therefore the Facilitator's responsibility to organise the venue and to determine the layout. However, all too often, the client has *pre-booked* the venue and the layout is therefore compromised.

> *Once when I was facilitating a strategy event with a Board they chose an ancient golf clubhouse as the venue. The room they were allocated was ornate and highly decorated with antiques everywhere! Hopeless! Another occasion a government department had booked the official residence of one the Government Ministers. We were not allowed to put anything on the walls of the Library, which we had been allocated! It meant bringing in several portable wall dividers at extra cost and they were in no a substitute for real 'walls'.*

So what should a Facilitator be looking for in a venue?

Size

They need to have a room, which is *at least 1½ times the 'normal' size.* When a venue says that a room will hold 20 people you will need one that will hold 30. Venues describe things in 'horseshoe'; 'boardroom' and 'theatre style'. Hardly ever do they include 'cabaret style'. Therefore, a good rule of thumb is to multiply the number of participants by 1½ and ask for a room for that number of people – remembering of course to keep the right numbers for the catering! An ex PE teacher recommended another rule of thumb which was for each person to have the equivalent space to be able to rotate with their arms stretched out. It is not that *they* personally need all that space but when added together it seems to make the mathematics of room size work.

Walls

It seems a strange thing to say that the room must have *'walls'* but process requires people to move around and to display information on the wall. A wall is therefore not a wall if it has pictures hanging on it; alcoves; furniture up against it; windows, which have fixed blinds; doors and screens hanging down or fixed to the wall. Yet you require all kinds of ingenious language and plenty of feedback when you speak to the venue to ascertain what the walls are like!

> *You must also be able to 'stick' things on the wall! It seems obvious but I once facilitated an event at a prestigious British University only to be told that the walls were part of the antiquity of*

the building and under no circumstances could we 'stick' anything on them. The fact that they 'sold' this room as a conference/meeting room did not seem to enter their thinking!

So beware, and ensure that you ask penetrating questions to avoid the pitfalls. 'Walls' will be your biggest 'bug-bear' and you will still get caught out. Even though you think that you have asked every question and checked all the 'angles', sadly you will arrive to find that the (several) windows are 'bay' windows and that you can not use them to stick flip chart paper on as you had intended!

Tables

Ah yes, tables, another thing to ruin a facilitator's day! They come in all shapes and sizes and yet often they are either cumbersome or fixed to the floor or fixed in shape and size. Effective process requires groups to be able to sub-divide, to work in different combinations of people and yet rooms and tables are invariably designed for the *One to All* format and nothing else!

One of my great successes was to convince a management team to sell the antique table, which adorned their main meeting room. They came to see that despite it being an attractive piece of furniture it was useless for the type of meetings and process that they had begun to appreciate.

Ideally, tables need to be capable of sub-division or, conversely, of being able to be fitted together to make a larger table, if required.

Flip charts and pens

Asking for more than one flip chart seems to throw venues into complete confusion. It is a bit like in Charles Dicken's "Oliver Twist" when Oliver has the nerve to ask for more gruel. The person running the Workhouse says "Moreeee!" in indignation as no one had *ever* done this before. When you ask for several flip charts, one per group, you get a similar reaction. You're lucky if you get a complete set of marker pens for *each* flip chart. Therefore, the facilitator should carry a personal set of large markers.

Kit

A good facilitator *always* carries a kit around with them. Just like a doctor, you never know when you will be required to act in your role. So what is in a *Facilitator's Kit Bag?*

It should contain the following, as a minimum:

- *Post Its™* - at least three sizes (for capturing issues of different subsiduarity); at least four different colours (for capturing different themes); at least four different shapes (you can print them from

WORD and use picture spray holder to attach them to the flip chart paper).

- *Marker pens* – large ones, in four colours for each flip chart and thinner ones, one for each person for writing on Post Its™.
- *Repertory Grid Forms* (see page 146) and *Relative Importance Grid*[3] - master copies which you can photocopy for use in an *All* format.
- *Dots* - at least three sizes (for prioritising issues of different subsiduarity); at least four different colours (for prioritising different themes); at least four different shapes (for marking different contexts).
- *Blu-Tac™* or equivalent – one 'lump' per table (if you do not provide it *on the table* dysfunctional groups *will not* put their flip chart paper on the wall but instead just turn over the sheets.
- *Spray* – to join pieces of (flip chart) paper together to make matrices and action planning sheets (there is nothing worse than action planning on a portrait flip chart stand). Why do they not make landscape flip chart stands?
- *Photos/artefacts* – brainstorming is much more effective if you have artefacts and photos to stimulate people's imagination. These can either be physical or on your laptop and be displayed as a 'filmstrip'.
- *String* – different thicknesses and possibly different colours. This may seem an odd material to suggest carrying around. However, you may find that it comes in useful when you need to connect themes or individual issues on a wall chart or in tasks such as 'stakeholder mapping' when you need to link different stakeholders in different ways (e.g. strong relationship – thick string; weak relationship – thin string).
- *Digital camera* – indispensable for capturing data and avoiding the client having to take the flip chart paper, back to the office or to have it typed up into an inappropriate format such as WORD. It enables information to be sent to people in its original format, thus maintaining the memory of the event and the dynamics of the situation.
- *Video camera* – think about using a video camera to capture key presentations by the (sub) groups and to preserve the dynamics of the occasion. Often presenting information in this way can be much more 'vivid' and powerful than translating the data into WORD, Excel or PowerPoint.

---

[3] Facilitation – A Handbook of Models, Tools and Techniques for Effective Group Work by the same author - ISBN 978 0 9556435 1 4 p.142

The Art, Science and Skill of Facilitation

This may suggest that your 'kit bag' is very big (and heavy) but you are, after all, going to have a number of people engaged in an activity which could, if it goes well: save a lot of money; establish a new way of working; solve a long-standing problem or create a new innovative solution. It is worth having the right materials, kit and equipment if that is the outcome.

Chapter Five – Process Iceberg® Model
- o Process Iceberg Model® explained
- o Dealing with problems in meetings
- o Using SCA and SPO – inner dialogue
- o Thinking 'up and down' the Iceberg and 'forward'

Process Iceberg® explained
At the heart of this approach to facilitation, lies the Process Iceberg® Model (see Diagram 1 below). It provides an explanation of much of what happens in group dynamics', in meetings/events' organisations and change. The Process Iceberg® is both a theoretical model and a practical way of auditing situations. The Model is:
- - *hierarchical:* each level has to be in place before the next one comes into play
- - *sequential:* each layer follows on from the previous one
- - *inter-dependant:* each level relies on the level above

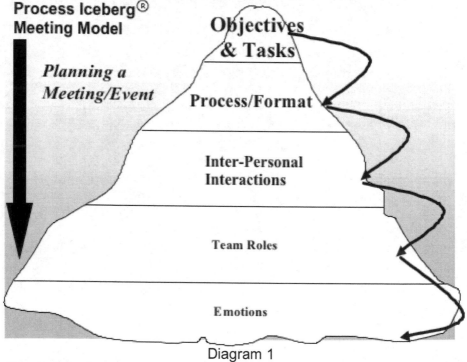

Diagram 1

Hierarchical
The Process Iceberg® Model presumes that the group will know or define the objective and IF they do that then the process and format will consequently follow. The objective and the process/format are symbiotic (see page 7). The process and format must 'fit' the task and the Facilitator matches them to ensure that they will deliver the expected outcomes. IF the objective is defined and the process and format have

been designed to match the need then (in Pareto terms) 80% of the difficulties of managing a meeting will have been absorbed. Put another way only 20% of the issues, which arise in meetings/events, are caused by factors *outside* this (see Diagram 2).

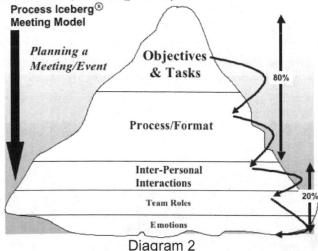

Diagram 2

Examine this sentence for a moment: *"IF the objective is defined and the process and format have been designed to match the need then (in Pareto terms) 80% of the difficulties of managing a meeting will have been absorbed".* The inference here is that *most* of the problems in meetings/events are caused by the failure to clearly identify and clarify the *objective* and the failure to use an effective *process* and *format*. Return to the hypothetical factory. They know *what* they are producing and the *process* is fixed. That is, how they can maximise efficiency and reduce wastage. Many (management) meetings fail to identify clearly the objective (probably because it is *uncertain)* and *process* is alien to many groups/teams. Therefore, the Facilitator's role is primarily to help the group define the objective by using a suitable process. Invariably one of the key ways for doing this is the Feedback Model.

Sequential
The Facilitator should focus their efforts on each *subsequent* level of the Process Iceberg®. If the objective is well defined and the process and format 'fit' the tasks then there will be much *less* pressure on the *inter-personal* skills. If everyone understands the objective and recognises that the process *will* deliver the outcomes required then the conversation/debate/discussion will be 'managed' and focused. If this is in place then people's personal *team role/personality type* will be positively harnessed and contribute to the outcome. A good Facilitator will have designed the process and used the appropriate format to meet the task needs *and* to balance and maximise the individual's input. If this

is all in balance, then people's *emotions* will be neutral and people will be able to concentrate on the task in hand. By 'neutral' it does not mean, dull or inactive, rather it means that people will neither be hyper-excited or negative and hostile.

Inter-dependant

Each level of the Process Iceberg® Model is *inter-dependant.* In the previous paragraph the key word was *'if'.* IF all the levels are in place then the Facilitator has made a conscious effort to work 'down' through the levels. The group/team will then find tackling the Objective much easier. Each level is dependant on the level above having been actioned and being 'in place'.

Objective and Process/Format

The very first thing that a group needs to do is to spend time defining the *objective*. It is frightening to say, "We have to spend the first hour defining what we're going to define".   The Facilitator needs to give them the courage that it is okay to spend time looking at the very objective itself and to legitimise the need to spend time identifying the objective. Therefore, the first thing that the Facilitator has to do is to define a *process* and a *format* that will enable the group to find the objective. In 'Uncertainty' the first thing that a group has to learn to rely on, and a facilitator has to encourage a group to rely on, is that they have a robust enough *process* and *format* to find the question. That they can spend time working in 'Uncertainty' not knowing what the question is yet but confident enough that they have actually got a mechanism for finding the question. If you were going to walk across very soft snow, you would probably want to wear snowshoes that spread your weight. These snowshoes would give you a larger footprint than your normal shoe would and they enable you to walk across what otherwise would be impossible terrain because you can spread the load of your body. That is the nature of a Process and Format, it has to be designed so that it prevents the group from 'falling' down through the snow, it enables it to 'walk across the top' until they define the Objective. The role of a facilitator is to devise a process until the question begins to solidify, until they get onto firm ground. That process has to carry them all the time until they reach that point.

Inter-personal interactions

One of the other most powerful interpersonal skills that the group can use is analogies. An 'analogy', like snowshoes going over snow, is a way of trying to explain 'Uncertainty' before the group knows the question. It translates difficult concepts and ideas into 'pictures' that people can connect with. In addition, using Feedback and SPO will help the group check understanding and build common purpose.

Team Roles

The next important thing is to ensure the balance of the people's team roles, to ensure that the group is not over emphasising any particular aspect. Those of you who use Belbin or Myers-Briggs will know that if there is a predominance of 'Ideas people' in the meeting then the likelihood is all you are going to get is ideas. If there is a predominance of 'ISTJs' the group is likely to drive on through in one particular direction hoping that it's the right one, without doing a lot of exploration around the issue or solution. There has to be a balance of the team roles. However, it is unlikely that in any naturally formed team/group that the team roles/personality types are balanced. The Facilitator should take account of this likelihood by designing a flexible, adaptable, multi-type process that allows *every* type to maximise their input (see the photograph at the start of Chapter 3).

Emotions

All of the above is to ensure that the group is in neutral *emotion*, in other words that people are not getting frightened, get angry, disturbed or aggressive, nor that they're getting too excited. There is nothing wrong with people being enthused in a group, feeling good about what they are doing and in that sense excited about the potential. There was a famous company in the United Kingdom, which produced vacuum cleaners, and it ran a marketing campaign that if you bought a machine you could get a trip to America. It was a marketing and financial disaster, which ended in a number of complaints because people had found they were not able to get the flight they wanted and were very unhappy. Maybe, when that marketing campaign was put in place, there was a great deal of excitement and enthusiasm and there was not enough challenge and critical examination of the consequences of the decision. The emotions were not neutral, they were over balanced: too much emphasis on 'Oh this will be good' rather than on 'let's examine this, let's look at this carefully.' So even in 'Uncertainty' people should be supported by good process so that they can keep calm and tackle the task without feeling frightened, without feeling unduly negative about it, and without feeling so worried or excited that they go off in the wrong direction. Therefore, the function and the responsibility of a Facilitator is to:
- design an effective Process to achieve the Objective
- use an appropriate Format that will enable people to feel secure
- ensure that the individuals in the group are using their interpersonal skills effectively

- ensure that the team roles are balanced and any weaknesses dealt with by the use of suitable tools and techniques

in order that the people do not get over emotional.

Dealing with problems in meetings

If the Facilitator notices something amiss, in the way the group is working, then they need to use the tool: *SCA – Symptom, Cause, Action.* People's anger, resentment, frustration, worry, silence, excessive talking, bickering, arguing, nervousness, willingness to please, desire to compromise, forcefulness (the list is endless!) is only a *symptom* and the Facilitator's role is to identify *where* in the Process Iceberg® it has happened. The Facilitator should assume that there are 'no difficult people' and that people have the best intentions to make meetings and events work. IF the Facilitator has planned the meeting well then they will have done much to reduce people's angst. However, particularly in *uncertainty* there will be occasions when even the best-planned event erupts!

The Facilitator should assume that *every* emotion is *only* a *symptom* of a problem *higher up the 'Iceberg'* (see Diagram 3 below).

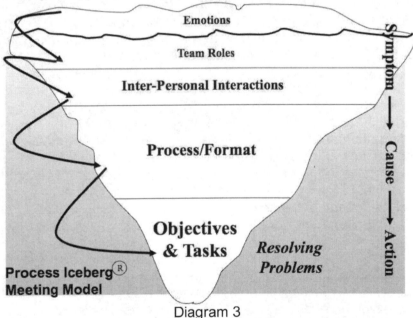

Diagram 3

If you turned the Process Iceberg® up side down, emotional insecurity (i.e. raw emotions) is possibly a consequence of *unbalanced team roles.* Alternatively, it could be the consequence of poor *interpersonal skills* (i.e. people not explaining to each other what they mean) and using words that mean something different to other people. If there is an inadequate or inappropriate *process and format* this will cause the emotions to become very disturbed. If the *objectives* are not clear this would cause people's emotions to become raw. Therefore, the Facilitator has the responsibility to be constantly monitoring using 'SCA' and to use the 'SPO' tool recommend changes.

Unbalanced Team Roles?

How will you know if it is because of unbalanced team-roles? The most likely clue is that people don't seem to get along. The normal day-to-day courtesies drop away, people begin to bicker, and they find other people irritating and difficult to understand. This can be largely attributed to an imbalance of team roles/personality types. However, if there is complete harmony or unity and yet it seems 'unreal' or 'surreal' then also suspect that the types are too homogeneous. Myers Briggs research into group working suggests that similar 'types' will get on well but may not produce the best results. The research in Chapter 7 highlights the danger of 'groupthink'. This can occur when the members of the team are similar or when there is a desire to keep unity and to avoid unpleasantness. You cannot for obvious reasons change the group. However, as it suggests in Chapter 7 you could bring in an 'outsider' to the situation to add a different dimension or complexion to the group's deliberations. Ideally, you should have done that *in the planning stage* if you recognised that the group was too similar in nature or experience. Boards of Directors have to have non-executive members and the best balance is to have a mixture of specialists and people with experience. If the *symptoms* indicate an imbalance of team roles then *go up a level* to *Inter-personal skills.* Encourage greater Feedback and more SPOs. If need be, you will have to 'translate' between the roles/types. This is not as hard or as strange as it sounds. You need to become an expert in 'Type' (see Chapter 3) and use this competence to help different Types understand what the other is saying. If you suspect that simply 'translating' will not be enough you need to *go to a higher level* and change the Format to create a balance or to distribute the types - to have them working together or apart.

Poor inter-personal interactions

How will you know if it is because of poor inter-personal interactions? People become frustrated and irritated if they cannot understand what someone else is saying or if the meaning becomes clouded. They become confused and either try to compensate by asking more and more questions or by going silent and assuming that they alone do not understand. Groups naturally use colloquiums that are part of their culture. This can be a departmental culture (e.g. SAP, 'platform'), organisational (e.g. 'client'/'partner') or nationally (e.g. 'Being on the same hymn sheet/in the same 'ball park'). You, as the Facilitator, have the primary responsibility to ensure understanding and clarity. Depending on the (process) maturity of the group either you will feedback; *someone* should be invited to or *anyone* needs to start checking understanding and the group should be encouraged to use SPOs whenever they make a proposal.

Poor or inappropriate Process or Format
How will you know if it is because of or poor or inappropriate process or format? Generally people become unsettled and annoyed if the process is inadequate or the format inappropriate. They begin to 'lose their temper' and their anger may turn on the Facilitator or the Task Leader, or whomever they consider is responsible for the way the group is tackling the Objective. You need to act fast. There is a maxim in facilitation *stick with the model, tool or technique and if it is not working 'pull out'!* This is meant to be contradictory. If you believe that the tool is the right one you should encourage the group to stay with it (using SPO), if however, you notice emotions getting out of control then potentially the process is wrong and you should be flexible enough to adapt it (see Facilitator's Profile characteristics in Chapter 7). If it is not, you need to re-design it or use an alternative process/format. The master bread maker watches the bread, one day it is pale and under-cooked another day it is dark brown, this depends on the water content of the wheat together with other factors. In response, the bread maker adjusts the process to allow for these factors. You will need to be continually monitoring the process to see (just like a factory production line) that it is producing what you and the Task Leader expected.

Ill-defined Objective
How will you know if it is because of lack of clarity of the objective and tasks? People tend to show the strongest emotion if the objective is unclear. It goes to the heart of their (in)security. If they do not understand the rationale for the meeting or the objective is uncertain it can cause people to doubt their own competence (as they grapple to understand), and to feel inadequate as they try to assimilate what is being discussed or angry that they have been put in this position. This insecurity is heightened and made far worse if someone is unclear about the strategic direction of the organisation. When there is a lack of clarity people get emotional, they get upset and angry, they start fighting, not literally but they pick on each other. When there is a lack of clarity in a meeting, all the natural reserves break down as the participants struggle to make sense of the situation.

The Art, Science and Skill of Facilitation

Summary
The cause of any emotion is invariably at *higher* level in the Iceberg: team roles; interpersonal skills; process and format or the objective. The golden rule for the facilitator is to take the action, *at least at the level of the cause or, if possible, higher*. In experiments, people's emotions *'looked' different* at *different levels of the Iceberg.* The emotional response gets more sever *the higher up the Iceberg the Cause.* You will *see* the symptoms and you should look for the cause at the *levels above*. You should then take the *Action* that is appropriate to remedy the Cause. The facilitator uses SCA as an analytical tool.

Using SCA and SPO – Inner Dialogue
A good Facilitator has an inner dialogue as they observe the meeting:

"What are the symptoms …. everything is alright ….. everybody's interacting effectively, nobody's particularly over excited, there's no rashness about the way that people are dealing with the tasks. … There's no frustration, everybody's quite quiet, that person over there is quiet – I wonder if they've got a problem, no, no they're just thinking deeply about this, they're probably an introvert, they're probably intuitive, and so they're thinking it all through. They don't want to speak yet, no, that's okay, I don't need to worry about that …. hang on .. that person's gone quiet - they were talking just now, they were talking quiet animatedly and they were talking a lot, and they've gone quiet. … That's a symptom some thing is going on in this meeting. They shouldn't have gone quiet, why have they?...Ah, because that other person has just thrown a strong challenge to what they have said. This has completely destroyed their argument, so what has caused that to happen…Ah, it's because it's a totally different issue and the first person who was speaking can't see it's connection with their issue. They don't see how they can combat it because this issue seems now to be catching everybody's imagination. So, is it that the issue that they were talking about was irrelevant and that what everybody is talking through now is a key issue? Alternatively, is it that they are both relevant but that the other people have not seen it? Now, that person, I suspect, is a 'monitor evaluator' and that they have seen something that nobody else has and everybody else is being caught up in the obvious ones. I think I need to intervene and challenge the group that there are a least two issues and they should not drop the first one.

………… *'Symptom'* … person going quiet,
………… *'Cause'* different team roles - they have spotted an issue that nobody else has spotted, has tried to put it in, it has not worked

71

.... *'Action'* go right up to the top of the 'Iceberg' and say to them: 'Are there two or three issues here you should be looking at in terms of your objectives?'"

Do not focus on the individual person because that will only draw attention to them and if they're not feeling confident – there could be more problems, so, construct an SPO and say:

"**(S)** I think there is an item that is being picked up which is this....... and now the group has picked up this other issue, and I have a sense which they may both be important and I wouldn't want you to disregard either of them until you've had time to examine them. **(P)** So, would it be useful to the group if, instead of taking one item and discussing it to death, you thought about all the potential issues and then decided which one's you need to tackle?. **(O)** That way you will be sure to tackle *everything that* is important.

This takes the emphasis off that individual but still gives the group the necessary support to alleviate the emotional symptoms (see Appendix 1 - 16. SCA).

Thinking 'up and down' the Iceberg and looking 'forward'
A good Facilitator will be 'scanning' up and down the levels of the Process Iceberg. They will be assessing the nature of the task to see if it is 'stable', that is, not becoming more uncertain or diversifying. They will be auditing the process and format to see if it is delivering the intended output. They will be watching over the Feedback to check understanding and buy-in. They will be discerning people's team roles and types to see if there is compatibility and integration or lack of harmony and conflict. They will be looking for (emotional) symptoms to see if they have missed anything. All this, while they are also looking ahead (with the Task Leader) to the output of the current process and the next task at how they might need to re-evaluate the objective and tasks and re-design the intended process to match the outcome from this phase (see Diagram 4). Sometimes there will be more data than expected or sometimes it will suggest different 'paths'. Sometimes the outputs will not be of the 'quality' or detail that may be needed or they may be too detailed. The Facilitator is watching all of this as well as the dynamics of the group and their relationship to the current process and task.

The Art, Science and Skill of Facilitation

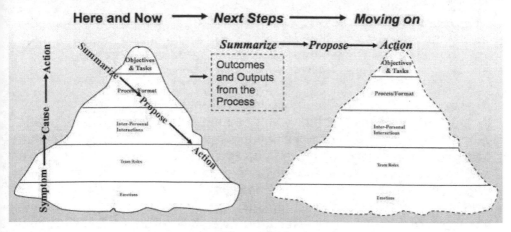

Diagram 4

Altogether, the Facilitator has a full time job. It starts at the first meeting with the client, through the design of the Agenda Format (Chapter 4) and contracting the style of the interventions (Chapter 6), into the event where they are at full stretch (Chapter 7) managing the delivery of the Objective(s) and harnessing group dynamics by (re)designing the process as required. This is no role for the faint hearted, nor is it a role for those who want to operate vicariously through the group. This is a 'servant' role, and a role, which requires great art, skill and a sense of the science of time and space.

Finally, the Process Iceberg® Model can be used at an organisational level using the same principles. The Model helps plan for change, implement a strategic intent and conducting a diagnosis of the organisation's problems. It can also be used at an individual level to explore personal (career) change. For more in-depth exploration of these concepts and their pragmatic application see the (forthcoming) book *Managing Participative Change - An Art, Science and Skill* by the same author.

Chapter Six - Contracting with an Group
- o Agreeing the Contract
- o The Role of the Facilitator in Terms of the Process
- o Why the Facilitator Needs to Have a Contract?

Agreeing the Contract

In Chapter 2 we looked at the nature of the facilitator's role in comparison with roles such as consultants and trainers and discovered that facilitators 'live in uncertainty' and should aim to be 'process experts'. We also acknowledged that the style and the nature of the role alter depending on the *Degree of Uncertainty* of the Task, the *Level of Process Awareness* of the Group and the *Time* available to undertake the task. The 'contract' with the group would alter depending on these dimensions. Chapter 4 illustrated how the facilitator identifies the nature of the Objective. This was a crucial step in ensuring that the group sets a realistic period and is aware of the difficulties of working in uncertainty. The implications for the 'contract' are also significant and the Facilitator needs to gain agreement with the Task Leader (and ultimately with the group) as to their role.

To do this the Facilitator can use what is call the *Facilitator's Contracting Matrix*© which lays out systematically how to agree the contract.

Contracting with the Client

The 'Client' is the person sponsoring the Task and who has taken responsibility for involving the Facilitator. The Facilitator should guide the client through the process of understanding the task and the Facilitator's role. This involves a step by step agreement of the balance between the role the Facilitator will play and the responsibility of the group for the: Objectives, Process and Format, Inter-personal Skills, Team Roles and Emotions and the degree of intervention in each of the levels of the Process Iceberg.

The Nature of the Task (Certainty/Complexity/Uncertainty)

The Facilitator guides the client through a diagnosis of the *nature* of the task, to determine whether it is Certain; Complex or Uncertain. This does not necessitate an *analysis* and discussion of the task, which will take place in the meeting. The Facilitator uses questions from the left hand side, see Diagram 1, on the next page to help the client recognise *how* uncertain the task is. The Facilitator then gives a short explanation of the consequences of this in terms of *handling the Task.*

The Art, Science and Skill of Facilitation

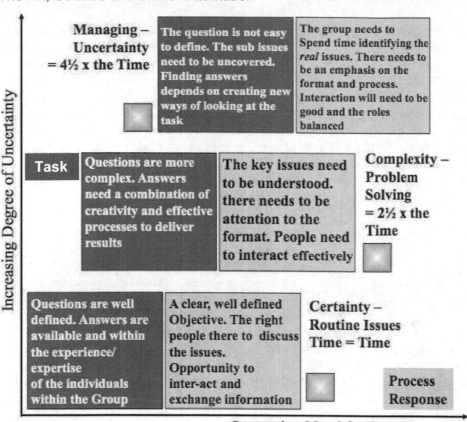

Diagram 1

The direct application of this depends on whether the Task Leader requires the Facilitator to be a *Key Interventionist,* a *Coach* to the group in terms of the Task or a *Responder*, which means the Facilitator holds back and does not make interventions unless asked to by the group. It is perhaps obvious, but important to say, that the Facilitator should 'negotiate high'. By this, we mean that the Facilitator needs the highest level of contract to enable them to do their job effectively. Empowerment of the group, letting them take all the responsibility in *uncertainty* (particularly if they are *dysfunctional* or just Transitional) would be akin to letting a five year old walk across a main road unaided!

The Facilitator must be prepared to take responsibility for Leading/Telling in terms of the Objectives. This does *not* mean that the Facilitator gets involved in the Task. They do not voice their opinion; they do NOT ask questions (such as "Have we enough resources to do this new product launch"). They simply feedback to the group what it is saying to itself and what the Facilitator is hearing. Certainly, the Facilitator should draw strands of conversation together (e.g. "I think I hear you, Jessie, you are saying that you need to allocate enough resources to this launch. At the same time, Bill, you are advising the group that this will mean pulling people off the Far East launch, and Sanjay, you are conscious of the need to pre-train anyone going onto that product. It seems to me that you have several separate but related issues here – I propose that **you** record them"). Just a note here the word **you** is in bold to remind the Facilitator that they are NOT part of the group and it is not *our* task but *theirs.* The use of *you* keeps that separation and although *'we'* sounds inclusive, (as if the Facilitator is the group's friend) they should not confuse guide and enabler with task participant.

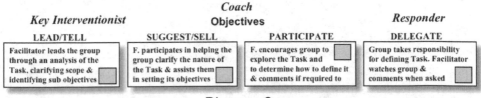

Key Interventionist	***Coach*** **Objectives**		**Responder**
LEAD/TELL	**SUGGEST/SELL**	**PARTICIPATE**	**DELEGATE**
Facilitator leads the group through an analysis of the Task, clarifying scope & identifying sub objectives	F. participates in helping the group clarify the nature of the Task & assists them in setting its objectives	F. encourages group to explore the Task and to determine how to define it & comments if required to	Group takes responsibility for defining Task. Facilitator watches group & comments when asked

Diagram 2

Diagram 2 above illustrates the different *type* of role that the Facilitator can assume. They can Lead/Tell; Suggest/Sell; Participate or Delegate. Again, this does not mean that they take part; a careful reading of the different options will show that in fact the Facilitator is simply aiding the group to find the objective and is NOT contributing to the discussion.

The Relationship between Time, Process and Task (The Facilitation Triangle)

The Facilitator asks the task leader how much *emphasis* they want to give to the Task and to understanding/contributing to the choice of Process, *given the time constraints* and the *nature of the Task.* This is important because it will determine the exact relationship between the Facilitator and the group in terms of 'green' thinking and *process* interventions. This dimension, more so than any other, takes account of the *time* element and the capability of the group to dual think ('red' and 'green').

This will help to determine the relationship between the Facilitator and the group (see Diagram 3 on next page). If the group chooses to focus on the task (1) then the facilitator will take most of the responsibility for the process. This would be appropriate if, say, the group was facing an operational or strategic crisis and needed to focus *all* of their thinking in 'red'.

> *On one occasion when I was working with a group of managers, they received two emails, one, which affected the strategic focus of*

the company, and the other, which had an immediate impact on the survival of the business. They needed to give all their attention to the issues and my 'contract' was to take responsibility for designing an appropriate process for tackle both issues.

If, on the other hand, the group decides that the task is not very significant they can give more emphasis to the process (e.g. discussing the best way to work, selecting the most appropriate technique). Alternatively, it may be a balance between the two. Diagram 3 shows the various options from, on the left hand side, the Facilitator taking *all* of the responsibility for process, to on the right hand side the group focusing on the process. Of course, to make this likely and realistic this would require either a) a non-important task or b) a certain task or c) a Process Aware group.

Agreeing the Emphasis on Task, Time & Process

Lead/Tell	Support/Sell	Facilitator's Style	Participate	Delegate
Process Task Time	Process Task Time	Process Task Time	Process Task Time	Process Task Time
Critical	Urgent	Urgency of the Task	Less Important	Insignificant
1. Task Predominates The group maturity & the urgency of the Task dictates that the F takes all responsibility for the for the Process	*2. Focus on the Task* The group may give prominence to the Task and ask the F to lead them through the Process	*3. Equal Attention* The group agree to give equal attention to Process & Task. The F's role will be to involve the group in the process	*4. Focus on Process* The group decide to use the opportunity to develop their Process skills even if the Task suffers somewhat	*5. Process Predominates* The group give their full attention to the Process, the Task is just the vehicle for achieving this

Diagram 3

Analysis of The Maturity Of The Group (Dysfunctional – Process Aware)

It is important for the client/group to be realistic about the group's level of process maturity. The maturity of the individuals or the length of time the group has been together is not a measure of the Process Awareness of the group. The Facilitator can ask a number of key questions about *how* the group works together on tasks to elicit a reasonably accurate understanding of the maturity level:

- do they use aids, such as flip charts/whiteboards?
- is there a 'set' leader and does the leader take the key decisions?

Contracting with an Group

- does everyone sit in the same place, does the group always work in the same room/environment?
- do they adapt the way they work to suit the task?
- do they discuss the process?
- do they review how they work?
- do individuals take responsibility for the way they behave and contribute

This is so important that it is worth developing your own 'matrix' for assessing a group's *process* maturity. The previous questions have been put in a matrix at Appendix 3 on page 200 to show how this can work.

The Facilitator should agree the level of maturity (Dysfunctional/ Transitional/Process Aware) that the diagnosis reveals and explain what that will mean in terms of the relationship between the Facilitator and the group and the function of the Facilitator (see Diagram 4 below).

Relationship between Facilitator's Role & Group's Maturity

Functional	Transitional	Process Aware
The group is only able to tackle Tasks in Certainty. There is a marked absence of *process skills*. A Complex or Uncertain situation causes the Group problems, emotions can run high and success is patchy	The Group becomes aware of the impact of the *Process* in achieving the Task. The Group is beginning to recognise Complexity and Uncertainty and to adopt different formats to tackle the task. It takes more responsibility for Process	The Group is able to face Uncertainty uses a wide variety of Process skills to achieve the Task. Success is frequent and the Group knows why it succeeds. Each individual takes personal responsibility for Process injects
←0%		100%→
The Facilitator takes a strong lead in helping the Group to define the Task, creating a suitable Format, guiding inter-personal exchanges, so that it achieves the Task and improves its *Process Awareness*	The Facilitator guides the Group helping it to take more responsibility for all aspects of the *Process*. The facilitator is, However, ready to take the lead if the Group needs greater input	The Facilitator operates as an observer and does not interject without permission from the Group. The Facilitator gives input when asked and provides feedback when requested to by the Group
Key Interventionist	Coach	Passive Responder

Diagram 4

The Role of the Facilitator in Terms of the Process
Setting the 'style' in which the Facilitator will operate follows on from this analysis. It will be based on the combination of: the *degree of uncertainty of the task,* the *level of process awareness and* the *time available.*

Process and Format
The Facilitator is inviting the group to decide how much responsibility they feel that they can take for the *process.* Here the Facilitator must be

careful to ensure that the group does not a) abdicate all responsibility for process or b) take on more responsibility than it can handle. You can demonstrate the dynamic by asking two people to hold each other by one hand and lean back. Both must take the strain (as they do in a tug-of-war). If one lets go the other will fall over. It is the same in managing the process, both the Facilitator and the group must a) trust each other to take responsibility and b) take as much responsibility (and no more) as they can handle.

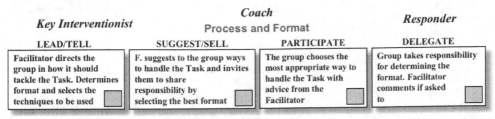

Diagram 5

The Facilitator should ensure that the contract is explicit and agreed (see Diagram 5), because the success of the Task will depend on the effective interaction between the Facilitator and the group. The Facilitator should suggest the most appropriate level of intervention if the group is Dysfunctional or ask the group to suggest the level of responsibility/intervention if it is Transitional/Process Aware.

Inter-personal

The next level of contracting is at the *Inter-personal skills* level (see Diagram 6).

Diagram 6

Some models of assessing and auditing group interaction feature a whole host of behaviours: supporting, building, proposing, blocking, seeking information etc. The difficulty with such a model (in a dysfunctional/transitional group) is that it puts too much pressure on the individual especially in *uncertainty*. Think about this for a moment? If the task is *uncertain* then the likelihood is that people's inter-personal skills (just like the pit crew's skills – page 91) will be sorely tested. If the process/format is wrong or inappropriate then it will put undue pressure on the individual.

I remember once, a very intelligent woman was struggling to come to terms with a Relative Importance Grid. She did not like numbers, feeling them to be too restrictive and analytical for the situation which she felt required a more 'intuitive' approach (see Chapter 3 for more on different types of personality). If she had been required to use this tool, she would have probably reacted negatively and her behaviour would not have exhibited supportive/building actions.

Look at the Matrix below. What is your view of Gunja and Felicity?

Name	Inter-Personal Behaviour						Total	Comments
	Support	Building	Propose	Blocking	Seek Info	Give Info		
Sanjay	1111 5	11 2			1111 5	1111 4	16	Definitely seems to work with the group to achieve objectives
Helen		1111 1 6	111 3				9	Helped the group to find consensus
Dick	1111 5						5	Another valuable member of the group – if a bit quiet
Gunja				1111 5	11 2	111 3	10	Caused the group to 'stumble' by the way they challenged
Felicity	1 1			1111 111 8	1111 4		13	Caused the group to falter as they Challenged almost every thing
Total	11	8	3	13	11	7	53	The group seems divided – those who are supportive and those who resist

At first sight, they look a disruptive element in the group. What about Sanjay and Helen? They appear to be supportive members of the team. However, IF this was the British Cabinet discussing the, so called, 'Poll Tax' (which became a disastrous policy) then you might wonder if Gunja and Felicity had not been trying to prevent the group from making a big mistake. What if this was the vacuum cleaner company mentioned previously? Then the people supporting the proposed advertising/marketing campaign might be seen to be 'yes people' and the group suffering from 'Group Think'. Individual's inter-personal contributions might be (adversely) affected by an ill-defined Objective, an ineffective Process or an inappropriate Format. Or, the lack of good Feedback, a failure to balance the weakness in Team Roles (to overcome the absence of a 'Critical Evaluator' or a predominance of 'Ideas' people) and the subsequent arousal of emotions which the individuals struggled to contain.

The message is loud and clear - when analysing inter-personal behaviour *always* check that the Objective is clear and the Process effective and appropriate. People's behaviour and emotion is *usually* driven by factors *'higher'* up the Process Iceberg. Therefore, 'keep it simple'; the primary inter-personal skill is Feedback (to which you could add SPO). If the Process and Format is right then all that people will need is good Feedback Skills. However, this is still a big ask of dysfunctional groups and even Transitional groups struggle to remember to feedback to their colleagues especially in the heat of uncertainty.

The key question then is "Who does the Feedback?" It is a trick question because it depends on the process maturity of the group. If a group is dysfunctional then the likelihood is that *no one* will give feedback. People *might* ask questions, some, including the leader, may well ask people to speak out but the likelihood is that *no one* will feed back. This means that the Facilitator *has* to take on that responsibility. To do otherwise risks the group becoming even more dysfunctional and people retreating further. However, if the Facilitator feeds back and they see the impact of it there is the potential for members of the group to recognise the significance and power of this tool.

If the group is Transitional then the Facilitator can ask for 'someone' to feedback. The possibility is that there will be a 'someone' who will feedback and as long as that 'someone' is not doing it to put their own spin on the speaker's words then the group will be the better for it. The Facilitator can say something like "I think John is making a point here about the way the sales process should be changed would anyone like to feedback what they hear him advocating?"

If the group is Process Aware then the likelihood is that 'someone' will take on the responsibility of feeding back what others have said. In fact if the group has matured this far then usually most of the group will feedback to others. It is even possible as the group becomes comfortable with the Feedback Model that individuals will ask for 'reverse' feedback (see page 31) and ask people to feedback to them!

So the answer to the question "Who does the feedback?" is a means of assessing the group's maturity. The Facilitator will get a clear indication of the group's maturity depending on who does the feedback: the Facilitator; someone; anyone; everyone.

Team Roles

The next 'Level' of the contract is the deployment of people's expertise, skills and person attributes (e.g. technical competence; presenting skills; Myers Briggs Type®) to achieve the Objective. The group and facilitator should use the Team Role/Personality Type indicator that they feel will most help them to understand the group's strengths and weaknesses.

The Facilitator is seeking to combine the group's confidence and level of process maturity. If the group is dysfunctional and unused to being involved in activities within meetings they may well ask the Facilitator to direct how they are deployed (see Diagram 7 below).

	Coach		Responder
Key Interventionist	Team Roles		
LEAD/TELL	SUGGEST/SELL	PARTICIPATE	DELEGATE
F. leads in helping the group to make the most of the different strengths and compensates gaps in team roles	Facilitator helps the group to use their strengths to best effect and guides them in over-coming gaps in team roles	The group agrees how best to use the strengths of the group and how to compensate for gaps in team roles	The individuals in the group know how best to utilise each other's strengths and to cover gaps in team roles

Diagram 7

This can be as simple as allocating people to groups if the objective requires sub groups to tackle parallel tasks. This can be a significant moment for a dysfunctional group – breaking into sub-groups. It indicates that people are prepared to trust others to have discussions and reach conclusions without *everyone* having to be involved all the time. It paves the way for the *Group* format to become part of the group's 'repertoire'. However, initially they may prefer the Facilitator to allocate people to sub groups and tasks, rather than the leader doing it or having to choose them. There is all the embarrassment of who picks who to work with and who does the picking. Once the group has seen how useful sub-group work can be they may next time, be willing to share the responsibility with the Facilitator. Remember always, the Facilitator's aim is to mature the group by best practice and good experiences. Ultimately, the group should know its process and task strengths and weaknesses and be able to decide who does what at what point. This kind of maturity will mark out a group as Process Aware.

Emotions

Finally, the Facilitator needs to get the agreement from the group as to how to handle Emotions (see Diagram 8 below). However, there is one key point to note here.

If the Objective is clear and well defined, or at least that there is a process for identifying it; *if* the process and format have been aligned with the objective and the group's capabilities; *if* the feedback is being handled and *if* people are using their team roles effectively THEN, emotions should be 'neutral'. People should be relaxed and comfortable and although the task may be difficult, the group should feel confident. So contracting who handles instances of emotion should hopefully be academic. However, there is always the potential for individuals to find themselves struggling to handle their emotions, particularly if the objective touches aspects of their value system.

		Coach Emotions			*Responder*
Key Interventionist					
LEAD/TELL		SUGGEST/SELL	PARTICIPATE		DELEGATE
Facilitator handles instances of emotion, manages conflict and takes responsibility for the way the group behaves		Facilitator works with the group in handling feelings and managing any conflict. Both parties take responsibility	Group handles emotional issues and begins to manage conflict. Facilitator interjects when asked to		Individuals take personal responsibility for their own feelings and manage their own emotions

Diagram 8

If the group is dysfunctional then it will ask the Facilitator to manage any outbursts or any lapses in emotional intelligence. If the group is Transitional then it may be able to share that responsibility and if the group is Process Aware then individuals will certainly manage their own emotions in an emotionally intelligent way.

Once, when I was with a group one of the members expressed how hard he was finding the discussion. He asked to be excused for a few minutes whilst he went outside to clear his mind. He saw it as his personal responsibility to explain the problem to the group and furthermore his responsibility to manage his own emotions. On another occasion with a group coming out of being dysfunctional in the throes of examining the strategy, the managing director who had been with the business since it began, at the end of a long day, suddenly got very angry and his outburst shocked everyone and caused them all to doubt if the process could continue. I rang him afterwards and he assured me he was alright – often the person themselves is more upset about what they have done than the 'victims'. At the next meeting he laid a large bag on the table and asked everyone to look inside – there they found huge water guns filled to the brim! The invitation was obvious, everyone drenched him, the whole incident was laughed off, and he went and changed into dry clothes! This is an example of a team truly coming into a Transitional state, even if it was a bit of a bumpy ride.

Therefore, the Facilitator's role is to agree with the group *who* will handle incidents of emotion, though how they will be handled can only be determined if and when something happens.

Difficult people

> *In my nineteen years of experience facilitating a wide range of groups and in a wide variety of contexts I have only encountered about nine difficult/impossible people. These people had no intention of conforming to the group norm and indeed were out to sabotage the efforts of the group for whatever reason. The point, however, is that I have only come across nine people.*

Most of the time people's emotions are intensified because of an ill-defined objective, bad or in-appropriate process, the wrong format, a failure to ensure understanding through effective feedback or the team roles being ignored or misdirected. People usually try to do their best. Facilitators who revel in emotions fail to understand the investment that people make in trying to tackle uncertain tasks, often with great courage and application. Please do not set out to enjoy facilitating emotional issues, rather aim to manage the 'levels' above that: Team Roles; Inter-personal interactions; Process and Format and of course the Objectives, you will be surprised how effective you can become.

Why does the Facilitator need a contract?

Chapter 2 examined the difference between the trainer, consultant and the facilitator. The first two have an implied contract. Indeed the consultant will often have a lengthy legal contract specifying the work they will do and the intended outcomes. The trainer publishes the content course and the learning objectives. Occasionally you will see information on *how* they intend to deliver the course in terms of learning style. The Facilitator has no such implied contract and their role is often shrouded in mystery and misunderstanding. Some facilitators get involved in the task. Some specialise in managing the 'group dynamics'. If people are to comprehend fully what the *role* of the Facilitator is and the *style* in which they are going to do it, then they need a 'contract'. This contract is binding on both parties in the sense that both should endeavour to live out their agreed responsibilities. The advantage of the contract is that the group and the Task Leader, who remember also has a contract with the group (and the Facilitator) in the form of *Tell; Sell; Participate* or *Delegate*, know how they can expect the Facilitator to operate. This should clarify any confusion and should give them assurance as to what the Facilitator will do.

If the Facilitator 'negotiates high', that is aims for the highest level of contract that they think they will need to manage the degree of uncertainty, the process and the time constraints, then they can release responsibility *if* the group accept more responsibility than the Facilitator had expected. This is the ideal scenario. The group begins to recognise the power of Process and starts to think 'green'. In which case a good

The Art, Science and Skill of Facilitation

Facilitator lets them take more of the role *as long* as the task does not suffer.

Finally
As each position on the matrix is agreed (see Diagram 9 below), the Facilitator describes what their responsibility and that of the group. To make this clear the Facilitator should give an SPO *on every selection.* The group may decide to change the level when they hear the *consequences* of the choice.

The facilitator then summarises the 'contract' and the responsibility of both parties.

The Facilitator should agree with the Client how the Facilitator's role will be introduced to the group. The Facilitator will want to ensure that the group understands the role. It is imperative that the group accepts the contract. Ideally, this will mirror the one agreed with the client. If not, the differences will need to be resolved. Then the Facilitator summarises the selected options, explains what that will mean with *real/pragmatic* examples and then summarise the relationship – all the time looking at the group members to see if they are in agreement and have 'owned' the contract.

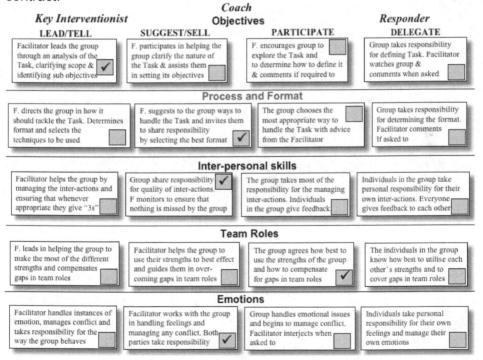

Diagram 9

Contracting with an Group

In the above example the Task Leader and the group have agreed that the Facilitator should 'lead' them in defining the Objective (which suggests that it is *Uncertain*). The contract also defines that the Facilitator should 'suggest/sell' the way of tackling the tasks by offering Tools and Techniques, using SPO. The Facilitator is sharing the responsibility for Feedback by inviting the 'someone' to feedback at any given time. The Team feel confident that they know each other's strengths, weaknesses and team roles and so they will allocate people to tasks and sub group working with advice from the Facilitator. Finally, the Facilitator has been asked to 'guard' the emotions and work with the group members to handle any lapses in emotional intelligence.

If you would like a copy of the *Contracting Matrix*™ then please go to: http://www.resourceproductions.com/models.html

Chapter Seven - Facilitating an Event
- o The impact of the Facilitator
- o Watching for the Causes not symptoms - Symptom, Cause and Action
- o There are no difficult people only a poor process
- o Feedback Model
- o Making interventions
- o Capturing information – drawing skills
- o Process Review
- o Assessing Group Maturity by the Process Review
- o How many Facilitators does it take to run a process?

The Impact of the Facilitator
Research carried out at Hamburg University[4] identified that:
- the higher the *quality of individual input* regarding subject matter at the *beginning* of the group interaction, the higher the quality of the group performance[5].
- the more *individual inputs are independent of one another* at the beginning of the group interaction, the higher the quality of the group performance[6].
- the more the group performance *includes individual input,* the higher the quality of the group performance[7].
- the more *comprehensible the individual input* is for each group member, the higher the quality of the group performance[8].
- *high quality individual input* influences the final group decision, the higher the quality of the group performance[9].

Therefore the conclusion was that the more a group facilitation technique enables the realisation of the above conditions in a group setting the higher the quality of the group performance and the more that comes closer to the optimum performance.

Process responses:
1) In order to increase the individual member's quality of performance, the specialized knowledge has to be elicited by a *structured and individual-oriented technique* which also aims to prevent social loafing and free-riding effects [10]

---

[4] http://www.uni-hamburg.de/fachbereiche-einrichtungen/fb16/absozpsy/HAFOS-52.pdf
[5] (Lorge & Solomon 1955; Grofman 1978; Sorkin, Hays & West 2001)
[6] (Sorkin, Hays & West 2001).
[7] (Hinsz, Tindale & Vollrath 1997)
[8] (Libby, Trotman & Zimmer 1987).
[9] (Littlepage, Schmidt, Whisler & Frost 1995).
[10] (Hoffman et al. 1995; Scheele & Groeben 1988).

2) In order to support subjective points of view independent of other subjects' opinions and under no influence of conformity pressure, group members *first develop their own arguments and problem solving strategy* without any personal contact to other group members. The facilitator should give each group member social-emotional feedback and motivational support and provide a common structure for eliciting the knowledge of each expert.

3) In order to consider all individual information, it should be exchanged among the group members in a condition which *excludes any normative influence*. Consequently all information will be passed on anonymously.

4) In order to achieve a high general comprehension of each specialized analysis of the topic, the facilitator pays attention to a *logical and clear explanation of thoughts* and opinions, of course without any interference in terms of content.

As you read the research findings above several things might strike you, if you read the previous chapters. Taking them in turn:

- .... *quality of individual input* regarding subject matter at the *beginning* of the group interaction........ and the specialized knowledge has to be elicited by a *structured and individual-oriented technique.*

In Chapter 1 we talk about *format* and the importance of selecting the most appropriate one for the situation. The *All* format can ensure that individuals are not intimidated by the other members of the group and that they can maintain their independence of thought as they move through the task. If the Facilitator recognises the dangers of one person dominating or imposing their will or opinion on others then they will select the most appropriate format *whatever* tool or technique they are proposing. For, hopefully, you will see that it applies to *any* technique: braindumping; Relative Importance Grid; using Dots etc.

- .... *the more comprehensible the individual input* ... the higher the quality of the group performance.... *first develop their own arguments and problem solving strategy.*

Again this re-enforces the power of *All* and the usefulness of *Group* to allow people of like mind to build their case *before* it is subjected to the scrutiny and challenge of everyone.

I learnt this early on in my career as a facilitator when, working with the senior management of a small specialist company I watched the managing director 'shoot down' any suggestions that he did not personally like. Nothing ever grew to a stage where it was a mature idea because he 'killed' it before it had a chance to grow! On another occasion helping the Scottish Football Association develop a strategy for youth football someone suggested an alternative approach in an aspect that the whole room was exploring. We were, I think, wise enough not to allow anyone to pre-judge his proposal, instead we asked him to make a two minute advertisement for his idea and then we invited anyone who wanted to, to work with him to develop the thinking. Perhaps you will not be surprised that the idea when full grown was fully endorsed by the room and became part of the ultimate strategy!

The Facilitator must 'slow things down', that is ensuring that the process runs its course. Anyone who opens the oven door when baking a cake learns, to their cost, that it will not rise correctly (that's why ovens have glass doors!) – we need glass doors on our processes, so we do not interrupt them). Anyone who interrupts a program downloading will ruin the installation. Likewise, the facilitator must ensure that the process runs its course and allows individuals to establish a comprehensive input.

- the more *high quality the individual input* the greater the influence the final group decision and the higher the quality of the group performance.....

The better the process used, the more appropriate the model, tool or technique the higher the quality of input and therefore the outcome. Facilitator's should use the 'right' tool or technique, not their favourite and they should be bold enough to encourage the group to work through difficult times if they believe that the quality of output justifies it.

I was working with an international group of Country Managers, as they tried to develop a pan-European strategy. I had proposed that they create a huge matrix on the wall and populate it. This took a great deal of time. Thankfully some took responsibility for the input whilst some sat back and watched the data emerging. After about 2 hours, even I was getting nervous as to whether it would indeed give us an answer (it was a bit like cracking a code!). Suddenly one of the managers who was sitting at the back rushed forward and started, animatedly, connecting bits of information and showing the group the 'pattern'. He had found the 'code' and the group went on to unravel the problem and it contributed to the overall strategy.

Good process will deliver high quality input and therefore good quality decisions.

- ......the facilitator pays attention to a *logical and clear explanation of thoughts* and opinions, without any interference in terms of content.

The facilitator's skill in feeding back (see Feedback Model) can help the process of sharing information enormously. Often people are expressing opinions and 'half-baked' ideas and thoughts, not because they are incompetent but rather because the task is *uncertain.* Ensuring effective feedback can help the individual and the group to uncover the real issues and fashion new ideas. If you have ever seen a Grand (Chess) Master going round from one board to another making a move and then going to next table and making their move and so on, it is an exciting and almost unbelievable skill. One of the greatest skills of a good facilitator is to be able to move from group to group and as they stand and listen to the interactions and to be able to give feedback which captures the essence of what is being said and even more to draw the threads together.

Managing Introverts and Extroverts
In order to integrate all high quality information into the final group decision the facilitator needs to minimize irrelevant influences e.g. extraversion of one person, the talkativeness of a (Myers Briggs) Extrovert or other social characteristics[11] and balance it with the reserve of the (Myers Briggs) Introvert. This means that the facilitator must become an expert in assessing people's team role/personality Type (see Chapter 3) and ensuring that each person is treated according to their Type needs. Introverts do not want to be 'picked on' and asked to speak. Rather, the process should enable them to input their thoughts. The Extroverts, can not function if told to 'shut up' and let others speak, again the process should manage their interventions.

Good process makes good decision making
The importance of the effective exchange of information facilitates objective evaluation and good problem solving. Furthermore, the collation of information and the subsequent judgment of the data by the whole group should be formulised by an effective process which enables the group *as a whole*, to select critical issues, identify probable causes, evaluate potential solutions and define a workable action plan, free of adverse consequences. The facilitator needs to use the best tools and techniques they can muster. They need to match them to the detail of the data being presented, the complexity of the information, the urgency of the problem and the seriousness of the situation. Different techniques like different artisan tools do different things and suit different situations – good facilitators deploy the *right* tool/technique at the *right* time and do it effortlessly and without fanfare or favouritism of the method or the individuals.

Principles of Process application:
A facilitative approach which adheres to the criteria mentioned above will in effect:
- maximise the *informational influence* on the group performance process

---

[11] (Littlepage et al. 1995)

- minimize the *normative influence* on the group performance process
- optimize the *influence of individual input* on the final group decision

Watching for the Causes not symptoms - Symptom, Cause and Action

Looking up and down the Process Iceberg® Model (see Chapter Five) and looking forward to the next task is a continuous requirement. The facilitator cannot take their eyes and ears off the group(s) for a moment and yet at the same time they need to be looking at the potential outputs from the current task and anticipating what model, tool or technique to use next. The facilitator should be looking at the symptoms, just as a doctor makes a judgement as to the state of the 'patient'. The emotional symptom could be indicative of something seriously wrong such as the objective becoming uncertain or it could be something as simple as the fact that someone has used jargon and 'lost' their colleagues. The facilitator should be constantly using SCA and scanning the group for symptoms and then assessing the cause and looking to take the appropriate action (in line with their 'contract').

Making interventions

The 'style' of the intervention will depend on the 'Contract'. If the facilitator has negotiated (see Chapter 4) an *Interventionist* style then their SPO will assume that the group will comply. This does not mean that the facilitator does not need to give the **S** or the **O**, what it means is that the SPO will be a directive. If, on the other hand the Contract is *Participative* then the Facilitator will give the **S** and the **P** will contain options. The **O** will serve to explain what each option will deliver. If the Facilitator's Contract is *Delegative* then they may merely give the **S** and invite the group to identify the **P** and the **O**. It is a good rule to:

- NEVER pose your SPO as a question "Is the group OK with what they are doing?" You are there to know! You will frighten a dysfunctional group doing that – they will imagine that it is a trick question. A Transitional group will want you to coach them. Not as they will perceive it, 'play' with them. Questions are for trainers and maybe consultants; facilitators should not use them.

- NEVER sit back and let things run, hoping that they will sort themselves out. If the group has negotiated a *delegative* contract with you then they should be on top of events and process. If the group is dysfunctional or Transitional then you need to step in earlier rather then later.

- NEVER be hesitant "I wonder if you might consider ...if you would like to..." The group will lose confidence in you – quite rightly, if you appear to be undecided about what to do. The SPO is your tool to guide the group and they always have the option to challenge or add to it.

There are no difficult people only a poor process

It follows from all that has been said in Chapter 3, 4 and 5 that there *are no difficult people only a poor process*! If you assume that maxim then you will always be scanning the group using SCA to see if there are any emotional symptoms and be examining *what* has caused it, rather than, *who* has caused it. In your career as a Facilitator, you will probably come across as few as eight or nine 'difficult' people. These people are intent on sabotaging the event and making it as difficult as possible for everyone else. All the other times, when it appears that someone is being difficult it will be a poor process or format which is causing the problem. When you deal with the process and change the format, their behaviour will improve and often they will be able to make a major contribution to the outcome.

Capturing information – drawing skills

If the contract is *interventionist* then you as Facilitator will be writing on the flip chart or on Post Its™ to put on the flip chart. Remember to give the respect to the information you are collecting and recording. Use Feedback to check your understanding (just as anyone should) and write it legibly, clearly and neatly. Learn to draw, not become an artist, but to draw shapes, artefacts (such as a telephone) and why? Because the *Intuitives* (iN) like pictures and the *Sensers* (S) like words!

Process Iceberg® Review

Try to get permission to undertake a *process review* at the end of EVERY event. If we go back to our analogy of the factory the *output* is determined by the quality of the *process*. The same holds true in a meeting or an event. If the process is good then the result, the outcome should be good. Therefore, get the group to take part in a process review so that they learn what (process) has helped them achieve a positive outcome.

1. Ask the Group "What has Helped in terms of the *Objectives* – in achieving the task today?"
2. When they have identified an aspect of process ask them "So what will *you do* next time?" When they give the answer write the statement on the Model (see next page) *in the appropriate place (on the left hand side)*.

3. Then ask the Group "What else Helped?" and when they have identified a process factor, ask them "So what will you do next time?" Write this statement on the Model on the left hand side.

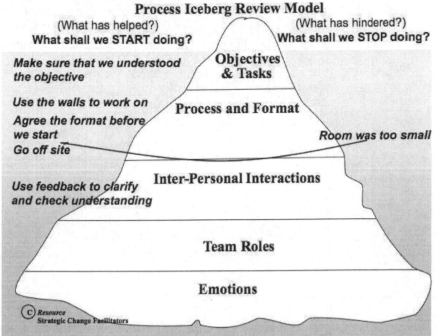

Process Iceberg Review Model

(What has helped?)
What shall we START doing?

(What has hindered?)
What shall we STOP doing?

Make sure that we understood the objective

Objectives & Tasks

Use the walls to work on

Agree the format before we start

Go off site

Process and Format

Room was too small

Use feedback to clarify and check understanding

Inter-Personal Interactions

Team Roles

Emotions

(c) *Resource Strategic Change Facilitators*

4. Continue to do this asking the same question *for each level of the Process Iceberg® (Process and Format, Interpersonal Skills, Team Roles)* and write what they have agreed they will do in the appropriate 'level' on the left hand side of the Process Iceberg® Review Model.

4. Then ask "Is there *anything else* that helped?" and ask what they will do next time and write that on the Mode on the left hand side.

5. If anyone mentions a 'Symptom' – that is something which is *caused by something else* – higher up the Process Iceberg®, (e.g. 'We were much more open today' or 'We shared more'), then ask the Group "What made that happen/possible?" and put the answer in the appropriate place *higher* up the Process Iceberg® on the left hand side.

6. Ask, "What hindered?" and write that on the *right hand* side and then ask "So what will you do next time?" and write that on the *left hand side, in the appropriate place.*

7. If someone mentions a negative emotion, e.g., 'We were very confused' or 'We ignored each other', write the negative emotion at the *bottom* on the *right hand side.* Then ask the Group "Wh No 1 would have made things less confusing?", "How could you have made sure that you didn't ignore each other?" and write the

positive actions on the *left hand side* at the appropriate level in the Process Iceberg.

8. If you want an overall measure of effectiveness of the event then put up a *Four Box Model* with two axes to represent *task* and *process* using words which will resonate with the group's understanding. Give everyone a 'dot' (using different colours if you need to see what different sub groups/stakeholders thought) and invite them to make a judgement about the event. Give everyone Post Its™ as well and invite them to write comments which support the 'score' they have given.

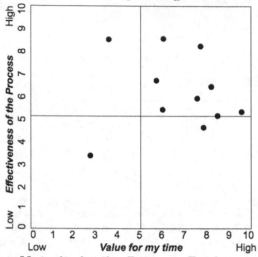

Assessing Group Maturity by the Process Review

You can assess a group's (process) maturity by the Process Review. Look at the example Process Iceberg Reviews below and decide which

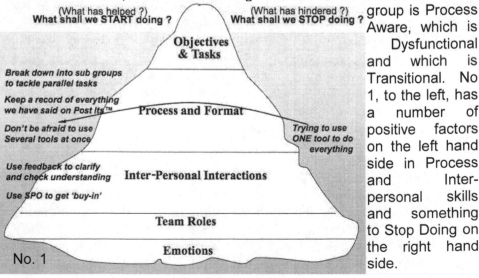

group is Process Aware, which is Dysfunctional and which is Transitional. No 1, to the left, has a number of positive factors on the left hand side in Process and Inter-personal skills and something to Stop Doing on the right hand side.

The Art, Science and Skill of Facilitation

Whilst No 2 has a number of positive factors in Team Roles, Emotions and a 'Stop Doing' on the right in Team Roles. These factors are at the *bottom* of the Process Iceberg.

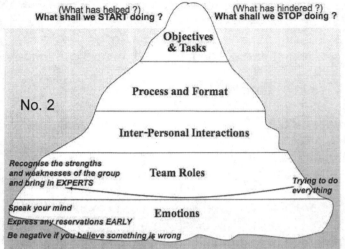

No 3 has a several things to 'Start Doing' in the Objectives and in Process and Format, together with things to 'Stop Doing' at the same two levels. The things that have helped and hindered seem to be at the *top* of the Process Iceberg.

Examine each Process Review. Which one is Dysfunctional? Which one is Transitional and which one is Process aware?

The answer is as follows:

No 1 is *Transitional* – the factors which the group is now identifying are *in the middle of the Process Iceberg* so they have already developed an awareness of the need to make the objective clear and have 'good' Process and appropriate Format.

No 2 is *Process Aware* – the group is so conscious of Process that the focus is on the need to better use Team Roles and the benefit of individuals taking personal responsibility for their Emotions.

No 3 is *Dysfunctional* – all the factors are at the *top* of the Process Iceberg suggesting that the group is only just learning about the importance of the Objective and Process and Format. Assessing a Group's maturity *after* an event can help determine the contractual relationship next time, and the degree of support needed.

How many Facilitators does it take to run a process?
The Process Iceberg Model of Facilitation is an interventionist one. It seeks to deliver effective process to match the task needs. It assumes everyone is keen to be involved and aims to find the most appropriate format, tools and techniques for *each* person, not *everyone* as a group. The Facilitator is there to design, adapt, change and manage the process to the benefit of the task, taking into account the parameters expounded in previous chapters:
- the nature of the task: certain, complex or uncertain
- the level of process maturity of the group: dysfunctional, transitional or process aware
- the time available to complete the objective(s)
- the number of sub groups the participants are going to work in
- the different individual (personality) types

Taking account of such parameters a good Facilitator can manage two to three 'tables' of six to eight people, *depending* on the uncertainty of the task, the level of process maturity and the time available. As the number of participants rises, as the degree of uncertainty increases and depending on the level of maturity of the group and the time available then additional Facilitators will be required to co-facilitate. On one assignment involving 27 managers who were at best transitional and sometimes dysfunctional, tackling an uncertain task, when they needed to break into different combinations of sub groups, from three to six people in each, with very limited time, there were three support facilitators, one lead Facilitator and the Task Leader.
The following Tables provide a means of deciding how many Facilitators you will need to support a particular event based on a points system. The first criterion is the *Degree of Uncertainty*. The greater the degree of Uncertainty the more analysis the task will require:

Certainty, Complexity, Uncertainty

No of people	Points			Points
	Certainty	Complexity	Uncertainty	
2 - 8	5	10	20	
9 – 16	10	20	40	
17 – 24	15	30	60	
25 - 32	20	25	80	
33 - 50	25	45	110	
51 - 75	30	60	150	
76 – 90	60	90	190	
91 – 117	80	120	250	
118 - 153	100	180	300	

The second criterion is *Level of Process Awareness*. The greater the process maturity of the group the *less* support it will need:

Dysfunctional, Transitional, Process Aware

No of people	Points			Points
	Process Aware	Transitional	Dys Functional	
2 - 8	5	10	20	
9 – 16	10	20	40	
17 – 24	15	30	60	
25 - 32	20	25	80	
33 - 50	25	45	110	
51 - 75	30	60	150	
76 – 90	60	90	190	
91 – 117	80	120	250	
118 - 153	100	180	300	

The more sub groups in which people will work the greater the need for the Facilitator to move around to offer process support to *each* 'table'. In addition the amount of time that is allotted to the task is crucial:

Number of Tables/Sub Groups

No of people	No of Tables	Poi nts
2 - 8	1 - 2	5
9 – 16	1 - 2	5
17 – 24	2 - 3	20
25 - 32	3 – 4	30
33 - 50	4 – 6	30
51 - 75	6 – 9	40
76 – 90	9 – 10	50
91 – 117	10 - 13	80
118 - 153	13 - 16	100

Time Available

Total Points	Points
More than enough	0
Enough	0
Not quite enough	40
Much less than needed	80
Very limited	150

Using the Tables above it is possible to calculate the number of Facilitators that will be needed to support the event (see Table on the next page). It is meant as a guide and the Task Leader and the Lead Facilitator will have to make a judgement as to the number of facilitators depending on budget, the significance of the task and the availability of (good) facilitators. Two excellent facilitators are worth six poor facilitators!

Number of Facilitators Needed

Total Points	15 - 120	125 - 210	215 - 290	295 - 370	375 - 460	465 - 590	595 - 720	725 - 850
No of Facilitators	1	2	3	4	5	6	7	8

Chapter Eight – Characteristics of an Effective Facilitator
- o Characteristics of an Effective Facilitator
- o Exploring Your Personal Strengths and the Areas where you will Feel Most and Least Comfortable

Characteristics of an Effective facilitator

Some while back we undertook research into the characteristics of an 'excellent' facilitator. Using the Repertory Grid Model we Interviewed people who had used 'facilitators' in whatever capacity. We interviewed facilitators and we interviewed people who had 'been' facilitated. The resulting profile was derived from a review of the research data after it had been subject to statistical analysis. There were four clusters and eleven key characteristics as follows:

Reaction to Change
Summary

A Facilitator who has a positive reaction to change will be effective in helping groups to explore and will be able to help the group examine different options and different variables without themselves becoming unnerved by the questions and the *uncertainty* it throws up.

Change Orientated
A Master Facilitator will be someone who is *change orientated.* A high score on this construct will mean that you are comfortable with change and probably have handled a fair amount of change in your own life and have learnt from the experiences. Uncertainty will not daunt you, nor will not knowing what is going to emerge next. You will be able to model change and help groups to feel secure in an uncertain environment.

If you score low on this construct you will need to learn how to manage your own reaction to change. You will need to recognise that a group will sense the facilitator's insecurity and lose confidence if you are appearing to find the situation difficult.

Bold, Brave Risk Taker
When dealing with uncertainty there are no right or wrong answers, only questions which need to be found and understood. If you scored highly on this construct you will be bold enough to try something in order to help the group define the task and to identify the key issues and questions. You will be brave enough to take risks with the process, if in your judgment, the situation demands it.

Ideas Orientated
Sometimes the tried and tested techniques are not quite, what are needed to help a group progress. A high score on this construct means that you are someone who has ideas and can 'invent' a new technique or adapt one to suit the situation you find yourself in. You may never use the idea or technique again but for that occasion, it will prove to be just the thing to help the group move forward.

Speed of Reaction
Summary
A Master Facilitator will react very quickly to situations and be able to handle any crisis in the process or with people's emotions. This speed of reaction is somewhat like a para-medic who knows what to do and does it quickly and without fuss – when others around them might be about to panic. A crisis can emerge suddenly when you are facilitating and unless you act quickly, the group's morale and confidence can suffer badly. If your score is low in the area of Flexibility and Quick to Respond and Act it is likely that you are someone who likes to take their time before taking action that might be precipitous. You probably prefer to weigh up the situation, balance the options and select the best one in studied way. The difficulty with that approach is that you may not be given the luxury of time. The situation may demand a swift response and you may need to throw caution to the wind on the basis that some action is better than no action, or which is too late to save the day.

Flexibility
A high score in this area means that you are not rigid in your thinking and you can adapt to changing circumstances. You will not mind if one technique is not working - you will simply select and offer another one. If your score is low then you might prefer to have a pre-defined plan or process and to follow that through. The only disadvantage of that approach is that the situation may demand a different way of operating and you might be seen as being inflexible.

Quick to respond and act
Like a racing driver you are often faced with a need to react quickly, if your score is high you will be someone who can see a situation, weigh it up, decide what to do and carry it out in fast time. Depending on your capabilities, you may be able to respond almost instantaneously. If you score low on this aspect, it is probably because you prefer a more calculated and reasoned approach to situations and you like to think things through carefully before acting. Whilst this may produce a better course of action sometimes there is not time to find the 'best' course, what is needed is 'a' course of action.

Approach to Process
Summary
To be a Master Facilitator you need to be interested and committed to process and believe in its worth and value. You will to some degree have 'dropped out' of the task and begun to invest your energy, time and thought in process. You will champion it and encourage others to see the benefit of thinking about and applying process to achieve better results. If you score low in this area then you probably prefer to get involved in the 'rough and tumble' of the task. You probably prefer the discussion, to the format and you prefer to get stuck in to a task and get frustrated with talk about "how we're going to tackle this subject matter" – preferring instead to get on with the job!

Process Orientated
If you have scored high on this construct you are someone who enjoys the mental challenge of designing the best process to achieve a task and you will get a 'buzz' out of thinking through how you might tackle a task. Your mind will be, at least in part, on the process even if you are involved in the discussion and your mind will be split between the 'what' and the 'how'. You will enjoy finding about new techniques and find it exciting when other people value your process contribution rather than your technical input or contribution to the subject matter. If you score low in this aspect then you prefer to stay in the task and believe that you best contribution is to have your say about the subject. At worst, you might not even value the process and you might believe it to be a 'waste of time'.

Low Profile Catalyst
A number of analogies have been used in this profile. When talking about Low Profile Catalyst another one seems appropriate. If you score highly on this construct then you are probably like a sheep dog! Happy to stay down and out of sight whilst the group is doing fine and is working it's way through the task without difficulty and ready and willing to act when the group needs help and input about the process. If you score low in this aspect then you might be a sheep worrier! You might be too prominent and too much in the lime light and not able or willing to keep out of the way. Or the group might feel that you are too conspicuous and may resent your presence. You may need to learn the balance between being seen and not heard and 'going for a walk round the lake' – in other words, never there when you are needed!

Extrovert
The Myers Briggs Type Indicator describes an Extrovert as someone whose thinking is external. In other words, they think aloud and they

need to talk to make sense of what they are thinking. On the other hand, an Introvert is someone whose thinking is internal. In other words, they like to mull their thoughts over to sort them out and to do so before speaking. If you have scored high on this construct then you are more likely to be extrovert in the way you think and relate to the outer world around you. You are more likely to engage with the group and to be willing and able to express your thoughts without much editing and much preparation. This will enable you to respond more quickly to situations, as you will be formulating your thoughts as you speak. If you scored low then you are more likely to be introverted in the way you think and relate to the outer world and more likely to take your time before committing yourself to speak. This will mean that you will be more reticent to speak until you have completed your thinking process.

Reaction to Stress
Summary
Facilitating groups, particularly when the group might be dealing with uncertainty and may not be process aware, can be very stressful. As a facilitator, you only have the process through which you can influence the way things work out. A Master Facilitator is able to manage their own emotions both during the event, and afterwards. It is vital that you can 'cruise' and relax at opportune moments and that you can discharge the pressure afterwards and not carry it around.

Calm under Pressure
If you sore well in this aspect then you are someone who is able, as they say, "to keep your head when all around are losing theirs"! There will be occasions when it seems as though there is no way through the uncertainty, and the group may well be getting agitated. You will be calm, at least on the surface and be able to give an air of confidence that the process will see them through to a good conclusion. If your score is low then it is more likely that you are stressed in difficult circumstances and can lose the confidence that things will turn out OK. The group needs to be able to trust the facilitator and you in turn need to be able to trust in the process, hold faith with it and do not give up.

Low Level of Stress
If you are someone who worries a lot and if you find that you dwell on things and mull them over for hours or even days after an event then you will probably have scored low on this dimension. You are more likely to find it difficult to switch off, even if the event has gone well. You might blame yourself if things have not gone as well as you would have hoped. If on the other hand you find that you can let things go, that you can hold things loosely and not dwell on what might have been then your score

will have been higher. A high score indicates that you are able to release the tension and not to carry around any negative feelings. This is essential if you are to become a Master Facilitator.

Breadth of Knowledge
Summary
As a facilitator your contribution is primarily in the area of process and you will have very little, if any, to contribute in terms of the task (knowledge). In fact the best events to facilitate are those in which you know next to nothing about the subject. However, your contribution will be in making the process work well for the group. To do this you need a very wide knowledge about a wide variety of things.

Breadth of Knowledge
You need to be able to introduce process suggestions with examples from a wide variety of sources to show that the techniques have some foundation. If you scored highly then you are probably well read, you probably have a wealth of general knowledge and can give useful analogies, similes and metaphors to help the group see that what they are doing makes sense. You may be able to bring case studies from other sectors and areas of life but this will not be as a consultant but rather you will be able to show the group that their situation is one, which others might have faced before in some way. If you scored low in this aspect it is probably because you see yourself as 'specialist' with knowledge in a certain field. Or it may be that you like to keep abreast with the technical aspects of your business whereas a Master Facilitator collects stories, examples, metaphors and illustrations from a wide variety of sources. They do this so that they can assist groups to put their situation in a context – which might not have a direct business parallel.

These characteristics have been put into a questionnaire and the output from that produces a 360° profile. If you are interested in receiving your 'self' profile then turn to Appendix 5 or go to:
http://www.resourceproductions.com/facilitation.html

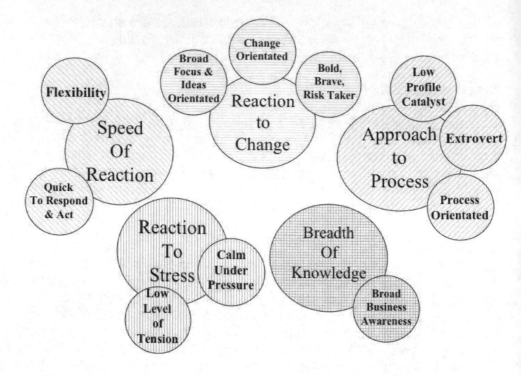

Exploring Your Personal Strengths and the Areas where you will Feel Most and Least Comfortable

The questionnaire produces a *Facilitation Profile* of the key characteristics (see below):

A 360° profile might look something like the one shown below:

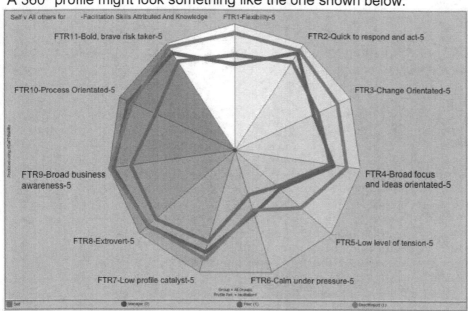

Environmental Context

The environment in which facilitators operate involves several key factors, which have an impact on the capability of the facilitator (e.g. 'Time' – having tight time pressures or having plenty of time). Applying the characteristics of an effective facilitator, *in the context of these external environmental factors* it is then possible to identify the *facilitator's preferred environment.* Using the scales below you can create a summary of your current strengths and *preferred arenas* and what you feel/think you need to do to 'grow' into the role.

RANGE OF CONFIDENCE - SPAN OF EXPERTISE

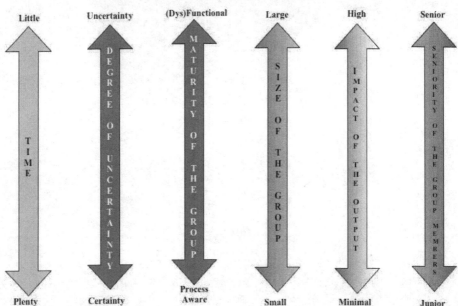

Taking each one in turn, you can highlight the 'range' and 'scope' of your ability. As in the example below:

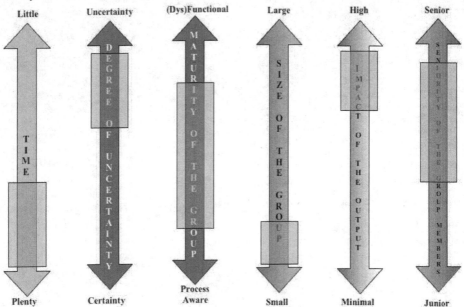

So a facilitator might, on thinking about previous facilitation encounters come to realise that:

- they actually prefer 'tight' timescales – the adrenalin keeps them focused
- they like being in *uncertainty* – there's more excitement in the outcomes
- they work best with groups that are moving into *Transitional* (away from dysfunctional) and once a team is getting *Process Aware* they cease to be a challenge
- in all of this they prefer working with small groups – large groups cause them to lose track of what's going on
- high impact scenarios give them most satisfaction
- they like working with more senior groups/teams because they are more comfortable in a strategic/longer term context, than the short term operational context (with all the issues of crisis management).

It would now be possible for this person to write a personal summary and to highlight their strengths and the environmental contexts, which they should either avoid or approach with caution.

Summary:

As an extrovert, I like being involved with groups. ......

Chapter Nine - Hearing the Process Words
   o   Hearing the Process words
   o   Exercises in hearing the words

Hearing the Process Words

Imagine that you have a friend who is in China on a year-long exchange to improve their Chinese. If they rang and told you that they had been dreaming in Chinese you would deduce from this that they were becoming bi-lingual. Gradually they had learnt to listen in Chinese and to form their responses *in* this (foreign) language – not their native tongue. The same is true in facilitation. Our natural language is *task,* 'red' thinking, we grow up fluent in it, having learnt our specialist subject (be it IT, Finance, marketing etc). We have to learn to hear 'green'. We must aim to hear that *first* not translate from task to process because the danger is we will get embroiled in the 'red' discussion and forget to think process. Yet it is not easy, we are trained to think about task day in and day out. So good facilitators learn to filter out the 'red' language and only hear the process words and then they are able to 'speak in fluent green'!

It is this skill that differentiates excellent facilitators from ordinary ones. Ordinary facilitators have 'favourite' tools and techniques. They like a particular tool and want to use it, regardless of the situation and the context. The technique may be good and it may work well but using their favourite tool without regard to the need, does not fix the problem, it does not make for a job well done! Excellent facilitators know which technique or tool to use, it fits the situation perfectly, and the group grows to trust the facilitator's judgement and to learn from them, absorbing not just the tools but also the context that goes with them.

So how do you do it? Well first, just as if you were learning a foreign language, you need to learn your vocabulary and the grammar. Just like an apprentice artisan, you need to learn what tools you have at our disposal and *how* to use them. Then you learn *when* and *where* to use each grammatical construction and how and when to use each tool. So the learning goes on accompanied by a growing awareness (if you stop listening in 'red') of the *process* words *behind* the red language. Just as an artisan sees the tool not the problem, just as your friend heard *in* Chinese, not their native language.

So how can you learn to hear in process language? Well first, you have to will yourself to stop listening in your native language. You have to trust that if you listen carefully the most appropriate tool or technique will become apparent to you. You need to train yourselves to recognise the tools and techniques and which go with which pieces of task. So for example if someone says, "I think we need to get to the issues here", then we should immediately think of Post Its™ and Braindumping as a starter. If the person says, "I think we need to get to the *real* issues", (my italics). Then we need perhaps to be using Post Its™ together with SCA or some other tool for eliciting the issues not the symptoms. If someone says, "I think we need to decide the priorities here", then we should immediately think of decision making/prioritisation tools such as Relative Importance Grid or Dots. Each piece of task has a process, a model, tool or technique, which suits it. You need to learn to recognise those links. Unfortunately, there is no 'dictionary' of process words, though it would be helpful if there was, as new facilitators would love to have one! You have instead to learn the indicators and the type of task language which indicates a particular tool or technique.

Below is a list of the advanced models, tools and techniques (which are described in Appendix 1) and a guide to the *type* of language and the context in which you should expect to recognise that they should be used. The Key Words should not be taken literally, rather as an indication of the type of 'red' discussion likely to be taking place.

Facilitator's Process Tools
The Process tools are the building blocks of a good facilitator's 'tool kit'. They provide the mechanisms to make other things happen. A good Facilitator is an expert in using these tools. To have the confidence to use them in the 'heat' of an event/meeting means using them regularly and consistently so that they become second nature.

Techniques	Situations	Key Words
Feedback	Feedback is used ALL the time. It is effective in one-to-one and in group situations. It is useful for clarifying technical inputs and for 'climbing out of uncertainty'. *There may not be any key words, which reveal the need for this Tool except a lack of understanding caused by a failure to use it!*	

SPO	Whenever you or anyone else wants to change the *process* and introduce another tool, technique or format. It is usually driven by a change in direction of the task, so you need to monitor the task and listen for changes in task direction/need.	
Analogy	Used when there is, for example, a specialist and you need to get people to understand what they are saying. It is used in conjunction with the Feedback Model. The clue to the need to use it is in the faces of the recipients and your own lack of clear understanding. Depending on your contract (see Chapter Five) you may have to invent/create an analogy.	
SCA	This tool is used when you, as the Facilitator, recognise an emotional *symptom* of something greater. This could be a personal emotion (e.g. frustration). In which case you will be looking 'higher' up the Process Iceberg® to identify the *real* cause and then deciding at what level to take action. Alternatively, it could be an organisational emotion (e.g. people not being kept informed). In which case you should use this tool to find the *real* cause and ultimately define the Action that the group needs to take to resolve the issue.	*Any words which are emotion driven or indicate a sub - cause* *"I don't know why this is happening"* *"It's not the real reason"* *"I think we are looking at the symptoms here"*

Data Collection and Issue Identification Tools and Techniques

The need to analyse situations, collect and collate data drives the need for these tools and techniques.

Techniques	Situations	Key Words
Four Box Model	Two independent factors, each with extremes at each end e.g. *"...It more about cost" ..."No to me it's about the benefit".* If you detect *two* different dimensions then listen for the 'pole' at either end of the dimension (e.g. low – high; minimum – maximum).	*Emotional words Disagreement over two different perspectives. Heightened anxiety. Raised voices as each seeks to influence the other's view*
Matrix Charting	Use anytime when there are multiple factors being considered as part of a whole. As with the Four Box Model, you will hear people arguing and see people speaking at cross-purposes as they seek to influence others to their point of view. If you detect *three* or more different dimensions, then listen for the 'measure' for each dimension (e.g. numbers/rating/%/words etc) – see the technique in Appendix 1.	*"I don't agree with you I think the first one is far better than the third and will give us more flexibility"*
Allegory - A Day at the Zoo	If the task is one, which might prove to be emotive for the group, then using allegory can help lead people gradually to uncover the issues. The task is one, which will be tackled more successfully if the group can 'distance' itself from the subject matter. There will be a need to identify the: *Now* and *Future* the *How will it be*	*"We have to imagine what this would be like" "Things have got to change"*

Brain Dumping	It is desirable to draw out from the group all the information that is known about a particular situation, action or event. *"There are a number of factors/issues which we need to explore"*	*Issues* *Factors* *Identify factors* *Ideas* *Thoughts*
Repertory Grid and What will I see Happening	There have been examples of a problem/issue, which keep re-occurring. This technique can be used when there are examples, which are 'good' and examples, which are 'poor' of the issue. *Good vs Bad* *Effective vs Not effective* *Positive experience vs Negative experience*	*"But we've got this right before….even if this time we haven't"* *"Surely it hasn't always been like this?"*
Restatement	This is used when the problem/situation seems intractable and a fresh way of looking at it is required. The problem may present itself as being quite rational but the solution may require quite radical and divergent thinking.	*"I can't see how we can solve this"* *"Surely there must be another way of looking at this?"*
Storytelling	This technique, like allegory, which it is based on, is used when the group needs to look at a potentially emotionally charged situation. It works when people are verbal (as opposed to visual) and if they are not good at writing (e.g. poor spellers) or if they are visually impaired.	*"We have to imagine what this would be like"* *"Things have got to change"*

Is and Is Not	This tool is essential when it seems hard to identify the 'facts' of the situation. It helps to identify differences and therefore distinctions. It is like Repertory Grid but is 'sharper' and cuts to the heart of a problem.	*"So what happened?"* *"What's different this time?"* *"Can't we sort out what happened?"*

Getting to a decision

The majority of us are used to thinking in a convergent way where we are using logic, reasoning and our powers of deduction to arrive at a suitable answer, solution or course of action. The following is a list of the convergent thinking techniques together with the situations in which they work best.

Techniques	Situations	Key Words
Relative Importance – RIG (see also Going Dotty!)[12] Going Dotty! (see also Relative Importance Grid)	The group needs to decide on the importance of a number of unrelated items. There are a number of issues/options, each of which has a particular value or importance to different members of the group. It is difficult for the group to reach a consensus on which one of the options is most important. *"Can we make a decision about the priority please?"* Whenever the group is faced with deciding: priorities; order of importance; order of action; who is keen on certain factors; stopping or starting action. Differentiating between different opinions.	*Importance* *Key* *Significant* *Crucial* *Least* *Relatively* *More important than* *"I think we need to agree which ones are crucial"* *"I don't see that one as important as you"*

---

[12] See *Facilitation – a Handbook of Models, Tools and Techniques for Effective Group Work* by the same author

Debate	When there is a need for agreement and it is important that the *best* decision be made nothing beats *debate*. However, transitional or process aware groups can only effectively use this tool. Strong characters would overpower members of a Dysfunctional group.	*Importance* *Agree* *Significant* *Best (decision)* *"I think we all need to agree"*

Action Planning and Implementation

Groups often complain that whilst they enjoyed a workshop "it didn't actually change anything". This can be because there is insufficient time and effort allocated to the action planning and implementation stage of an event/workshop/meeting. It is a time of hard graft and emotional when people have to commit to action and take personal responsibility rather than group involvement.

Five Questions – best used when it seems that the who, what, when, where and how could be 'plotted' (see also Linking[13] and Fishbone)	The group needs to develop an action plan or new methods and procedures for what is a well-known and current practice. The key to effective action planning lies in, *Who? What? When? Where? How?* However, we can also use this tool in the analysis phase because it allows the group to discover facts in a structured way: *Who did? What happened? When did it happen? Where was it? In addition, How did it occur?*	*When anyone mentions any of the key words* "Who, what, when, where or how?" *then it is an indication that all the words are significant.*
Force Field	This Model becomes essential when the group is about to embark on any action which potentially has 'fors' and 'againsts'. There is the potential for dys-functional groups to have 'group	*"Surely we can't ...if"* *"I'm not sure we can do it because..."* *"Is this feasible?"* *"I think we should*

	think' and to avoid facing up to the fact that the plan/strategy/solution is not feasible. Force Field can help bring the issues into reality.	*go for it even if it's hard"*
Process Iceberg® Model	This model is best used with SCA as a diagnostic tool. Whenever there are symptoms, the likelihood is that there are causes 'higher up the (Process) Iceberg®. *Any words which reflect the 'hierarchy' of the Process Iceberg® Any emotion/symptom words/phrases*	*"Surely we need to change the systems..."* *...structure"* *...training"*
Scenario Planning	This model helps to map the future strategy. It would be used when the client asked for help to develop a strategic plan.	

Meeting/Workshop Preparation

Preparation is crucial, setting out a clear pathway to achieve the objective and designing a process which matches the need and leads to useful outcomes.

Agenda Format	This is the Facilitator model for mapping the layout of the objective and designing the process to match it. It should be developed in conjunction with the client (Task Leader).	

Additional models, tools and techniques are available in *Facilitation – a Handbook of Models, Tools and Techniques for Effective Group Work* by the same author ISBN 978-0-9556435-1-4 (see Appendix 6), which is available through: http://www.resourceproductions.com/books.html

Exercises in hearing the words

It is useful to attune our ears to the process words and to develop the ability to 'hear' in green. Whenever you hear people talking in a meeting or in a business discussion then listen to hear the tools and techniques, you would use to assist the task.

The example exercises on the following pages are designed to give an opportunity to understand and practice the use of the technique known as SPO - Summarise Propose Output. The group's ability to recognise when and how to construct an SPO is essential if the facilitator is to help it to select the right technique for the right situation. The SPO technique is built around the fact that the Facilitator needs to feedback back to the group. This should be in the form of a summary of the situation, which they seem to be in, make a process and format proposal which will help them to move forward and demonstrate the benefits of this in terms of the outputs which will be achieved. The SPO technique is an essential tool in the Facilitator's toolkit. It prevents the facilitator FROM trying to drive a group into a process which they do not understand. On the other hand, it helps the group to trust the Facilitator and see how the process can help them. Facilitators who use this technique are much more likely to be respected by the group and both will enjoy the relationship with each other.

Situation 1

Ian "I'm confused. As far as I'm concerned the key need is identifying what the issues are and when we are going to take action. Some of the things we have to do now - and some of them are more long-term. I'm not clear which are the important ones. Some of the things that you're talking about, I think are very important and we need to act on them quickly. Some are not so important but nevertheless need to be done – (and that's why I'm getting lost)"

Christine "You're absolutely right Ian, I came to this meeting today thinking we were going to be looking at some of the strategic issues that we need to undertake over the coming two years……. and …."

Barbara "…What we seem be doing is talking about the problems that keep coming up day by day"

Tony "Hmm , It's all very well thinking about the long-term issues but I believe there are some very important issues that we need to address before very long otherwise you won't have a strategy with which to work!"

The Art, Science and Skill of Facilitation

Below is a template for you to use to think about your response to the discussion above.

SPO
Process Words - Write down the words which trigger process thoughts:

Proposed Model, Tool, Technique – Write down the ones you would suggest using:

Write your:
S:

P:

O:

When you have thought through your ideas look on the next page (or if you are an Activist look now!)

Situation 1 - Process Words and Process Intervention

Process words	The key process words are spoken by Ian – Ian … identifying **what** the issues are and **when** we are going to take action. Some of the things we have to do **now** and some of them are more **long-term**. I'm not clear which are the **important ones**. Some of the things that you're talking about, I think a **very important** and we need to act on them **quickly**. Some are **not so** important but nevertheless **need to be done** - and that's why I'm getting lost"
S	The way that you phrase the SPO and the degree of responsibility you take will depend on your contract. If you have a Key Interventionist contract you would be quite directive – if, on the other hand, you were in Delegative mode then you would simply offer your thoughts. Assuming that your contract was Participative then you might give an SPO as follows: "I sense that there are a **number of issues** floating around and you're saying that you first need **to identify all** these issues and then you're saying that you need to **classify** them: • some **urgent** some less so • some **important** some less so"
P	"I propose that you take a pad of yellow Post Its™ and **braindump** all the issues that you can foresee – regardless of whether they are urgent / important. Then I suggest that you post them onto a **Four Box model** with the following axes: • **Importance** (important to not so important) • **Timescale** (short term to long term) Then I propose that you use **Dots**: Red dots for *Quickly*; Yellow dots for *Quite Quickly*"
O	"I think that in this way you will get clarity and be able to determine what your priorities are and will have identified the ones which need to be done quickly."

	*You might suggest that if they want to further define the key issues that they do a **RIG** exercise – whereby they each complete a Relative Importance Grid and identify the issues, which they think, should take priority.* *You might also have thought that Christine was making a good point about 'Strategic vs Operational' matters. Tony suggested that if the operational issues were not dealt with effectively and immediately there would not be a future for the business!* *You might have wanted to **P**ropose that the group have two 'buckets' – one for (immediate) operational issues and one for (longer term) strategic issues.* *There are always several ways to tackle a task and that is what makes the role of a Facilitator so important and meaningful.*

Situation 2

Ian "As I see it, there's an awful lot that needs doing before the next planning meeting in two months time. Yet we all know what will happen - we will get to that meeting and nothing will be done! It seems to me that these items breakdown into areas of different Departments and individuals' responsibility."

Christine "Yes - I'd like to think that we had sorted out the important ones and then allocated them to the people that are most suited to doing them and that we could agree on what action they would undertake, when they would do it and any feedback that they were going to give".

See next page for the suggested response:

Situation 2 - Process Words and Process Intervention

| Process words | Despite the fact that there are only two people talking and the sentences are quite short there is an awful lot being said here.

The key process words are spoken by both Ian and Chris. Let's look/listen again:

Ian
"As I see it,   there's an **awful lot** that needs **doing before** the next planning meeting in two months time. Yet we all know what will happen - we will get to that meeting and nothing will be done! It seems to me that these items **breakdown into** areas of **different** Department's and individual's responsibility."

Christine
"Yes - I'd like to think of that we had **sorted out** the **important ones** and then **allocated them** to the people that are most **suited to** doing them and that we could agree on **what action** they would undertake, **when** they would do it and **any feedback** that they were going to give." |
|---|---|
| S | Remember the way that you phrase the SPO and the degree of responsibility you take will depend on your contract. If you have a Participative contract, your SPO would be in the form of an invitation – if on the other hand, you were in Delegative mode then you would simply reflect what the group was doing and you might simply offer a Summary.

Assuming that your contract was Key Interventionist then you might give an SPO as follows:

"You seem to have identified that there is a lot to do and that you need to be clear:
• **Who** is doing **what**
• **When** and **what** they will bring back" |
| P | "I'm going to give you each **20 dots** and invite you to allocate the dots to any of the activities you think are the most important. If you think, one is more important than another then give it more dots. If you think that the activities are all equally important then share your |

	dots out equally. Whilst you're doing that I am going to create a **Matrix Chart** which will have the following columns: • Activities to be followed through • Individual's (for people's names) • Department names • Action required • Deadline • Feedback to the group"
O	"In this way you will have **prioritised** the activities **allocated** the responsibility to named individuals or departments and specified the **action**, date and feedback required."

The CD ROM – "SPO Exercises" which is designed to give you an opportunity to understand and practice the use of the technique – is available from: http://www.resourceproductions.com/tips.html

Key Process Models, Tools and Techniques

No	Model, Tool, Technique	Page
	Process Models, Tools and Techniques	
1	Feedback Model (M)	125
2	Analogy (Te)	128
3	SPO (T)	130
	Data Collection/Analysis	
4	Four Box Model (T)	131
5	Matrix charting (T)	134
6	Allegory – A Day at the Zoo (M)	137
7	Repertory Grid (M)	140
8	Re-statement (T)	150
9	What will I see happening? (T)	153
10	Storytelling (T)	156
11	Is and Is Not (T)	166
	Decision Making	
12	Debate (T)	168
	Implementation	
13	Five Questions (T)	170
14	Force Field Analysis (M)	173
15	Process Iceberg Model (M)	178
16	SCA (M)	180
	Process Preparation	
17	Agenda Format (M)	184
	Strategic Analysis and Planning	
18	Scenario Planning (M)	188

This Appendix contains a range of advanced models, tools and techniques which you as a Facilitator will find useful in a variety of different situations. Some of these are essential to the art, science and skill of facilitation and will require confidence to apply them. Some take a few minutes to execute whilst others may require a whole day. In Chapter 7 you will have seen a quick aide memoir on each one, outlining the key (process) words linked to them and how to 'hear' process words.

Models

Models are the largest aspect of process. They constitute the key component of process. They invariably require the use of tools and techniques *within* them. They take time and usually match with an objective.

Tools
Tools are 'smaller' than models and 'larger' than techniques. They match with Tasks.

Techniques
Techniques are the smallest building blocks of process, which can support and be used within tools.

For a range of other techniques, which can be used, by facilitators and managers alike please refer to *Facilitation - Handbook of Models, Tools and Techniques for Effective Group Working.* ISBN 978-0-9556435-1-4, available by contacting the address inside the front cover:

Convergent and Divergent Thinking
When people in organisations come together they bring with them the barriers, different perceptions and established behaviour patterns of the organisational units to which they belong.

In the majority of cases, we also arrive having been conditioned to place great value on logic and reason in discussion and argument. Our collective brain, the **team brain**, is therefore likely to be thinking in a **convergent** manner.

Convergent thinking
Convergent thinking is what the majority of us are used to. It is logical, rational, reasoned and deductive. It is the process of making a decision. It starts from a number of possible answers or solutions and converges on the one, which seems to be the best. Convergent thinking is ideal for circumstances where there is only one correct answer or solution and when all the facts relating to the situation are known.

Unfortunately, in business and in life itself, many problems do not have just one right solution and not all the possibilities are clear.

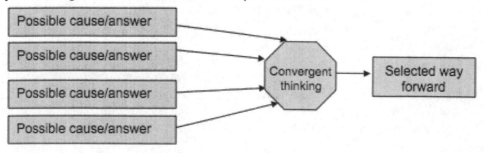

Divergent thinking

Divergent thinking is illogical and freewheeling. It is the process of generating ideas. It is slow and cannot be hurried. Teams using divergent thinking often need a great deal of time and frequently appear, in the short term, to be inefficient.

Divergent thinking is used most successfully in situations where there are likely to be a number of possible approaches to obtaining an appropriate solution, or when a number of diverse facts and circumstances need to be taken into consideration.

There are times when a group needs to break away from the more traditional ways of thinking, when people need to be able to view what is taken to be 'the norm' in different and new ways.

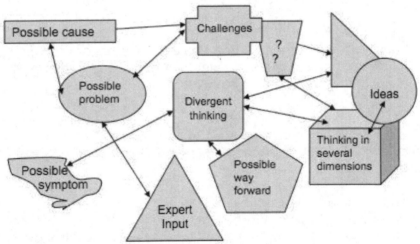

When working in teams a Facilitator needs to be able to think in both ways and to use tools and techniques to help the group to think:
- divergently to ensure that:
    - they have identified, publicised and agreed on the major issues to ensure that we are tackling the appropriate task or problem
    - have explored, generated and examined all the possible causes, solutions and courses of action
- convergently to decide on the best way to implement our choice of action or solution

The following Models, Tools and Techniques have been designed to help facilitators adopt both these approaches. They will provide them with advanced process models, tools and techniques to help groups work together more effectively in a structured, yet fluid way.

124

1. Feedback Model
(Process Model)

Purpose
The model should be used to promote higher levels of understanding between group members and to assist them in discovering the reasons lying beneath communication breakdowns. When used by all group members, it will enhance all aspects of their inter-relationships.

When to Use
The model can be used at any stage when understanding needs to be checked. Unlike questions, use of feedback is less likely to interrupt the speaker's thought processes. When groups are working in high levels of complexity or uncertainty, use of this model is essential.

How to Use
Level 1
Feeding back to the initiator or speaker but completely misunderstanding or misinterpreting what was said.
Level 2
Feeding back but missing some important points or interpreting some vital detail incorrectly
Level 1 and level 2 feedback usually occurs when the speaker or initiator is in certainty and the listener is in uncertainty.
Level 3
Feeding back what was said faithfully and accurately, preferably in different words, without addition or subtraction to the meaning.
Level 4
Feeding back accurately what was said and, in addition, getting behind the words to the real meaning of the message.

The facilitator should encourage individuals to use the model, always aiming at feedback levels 3 and 4. The speaker and/or initiator must respond appropriately to the feedback (e.g. 'No, that's a '2'. What I meant was . . . .')

The facilitator should encourage individuals to use the model always aiming at feedback levels 3 and 4. The speaker and/or initiator will automatically respond to the feedback (e.g. 'No, that's not what I said ...what I meant was...'). This will indicate that the person feeding back misunderstood what was said, BUT the speaker tends to take responsibility for the misunderstanding and goes on to say what they were saying *in a different way* to help understanding.

The facilitator should encourage the group to feedback as often as they can. One of the clearest signs that a group is operating in 'Uncertainty' is the failure to feedback accurately (i.e. to feedback at Level 1).

Words/Phrases:
"So what you're saying is...?"
"If I understand you..."
"Can I see if I have this clear..."

Reverse Feedback

Reverse Feedback is used when the speaker needs to know that the 'receiver(s)' have heard *and* understood what he or she was saying. In this situation, the speaker says something akin to:

Words/Phrases
"Can I just check that you have gathered what I am saying..."
"So what am I saying...?"
"I'm not sure how well I am putting this across ... what are you understanding from what I am saying?"
"I need to know that I am making sense! What do *you* think I am saying...?"

1 - Misunderstanding or misinterpreting what was said.
2 - Missing out some important points or some details
3 - Feeding back accurately and fully what was said
4 - Getting behind the words to the 'hidden' message

The Feedback Model can be seen as a 'bull's eye'. Initially the feedback could be a '1', which is almost 'off' the target. With each successive feedback, the person speaking and the listener are getting closer to the bull's eye – the core of the issue.

Alternatively, it can be seen as a set of 'steps' where with each successive feedback the person speaking and the listener get 'higher and higher' in their mutual understanding.

Level 4: Feeding back accurately what was said and, in addition, getting behind the words to the real meaning of the message.

Level 3: Feeding back what was said faithfully and accurately, preferably in different words, without addition or subtraction to the meaning.

Level 2: Feeding back but missing some important points or interpreting some vital detail incorrectly
Level 1 and level 2 feedback usually occurs when the speaker or initiator is in certainty and the listener is in uncertainty.

Level 1: Feeding back to the initiator or speaker but completely misunderstanding or misinterpreting what was said.

Associated Process Tools
Summarise, Propose, Outcome (SPO)
Analogy (to check meaning with different perspective)
Out of the Box

Materials
Flip chart
Paper
Marker pens

2. Analogy
(Process technique)

Purpose
Analogy is a technique for explaining something in a different way.

When to Use
It is best used when there is a need to throw new light on a problem and when it is desirable to adopt new perspectives. It can also be used as a part of the Feedback process to bring the understanding out of a specialist arena into the common language.

How to Use
1. Ask the group to identify and agree a clear description of the statement, problem or situation. For example if the problem is to do with a lack of downward communication, the statement might be "Our top managers do not talk to us".

2. Ask people to generate a number of analogies for the stated problem by transferring it to a different setting, one that is totally divorced from the real one. For example, an analogy for the situation in 1 might be "The custard doesn't soak all the way through the pudding, so the bottom is still dry". Keep using feedback to ensure full understanding of the analogies.

3. Encourage people to be as uninhibited and unrestrained as they can be. Generate as many analogies as possible.

4. Ask the group to generate as many reasons as they can for the analogies. For example, the analogy in 2 might generate reasons like 'the custard is too thick'. 'the pudding is too deep', 'the custard does not stay on the pudding long enough'.

5. Some of the analogies will be more successful and workable than others. Select those which are, (perhaps by using 'Dots') and ask people to generate as many ways as they can of improving the situation. Therefore, in our example, suggestions might include 'make the custard thinner', 'make the pudding less deep'. List these ideas so that everyone can see them.

6. Ask the group to take the solutions generated for the analogy and apply them to the real problem in order to trigger new insights and ideas about it. Prompt this by asking 'What do you mean by . . . . ?' In our example, a suggestion might be 'Make the organisation less

deep'. The response to the question 'What do you mean by less deep?" might prompt the suggestion that there is a need to make the organisation a flatter structure. Reinforce full understanding by the frequent use of feedback.

7. Once the group feel that it has run out of ideas, further techniques should be used to evaluate the suggestions made.

Materials
Flip charts
Markers
Pens

Time
1 to 2 hours depending on the number of people in the group and the complexity of the problem.

Associated Process Tools
Linking
Clustering
A Day at the Zoo
Storytelling

3. Summarise, Propose, Output (SPO)
(Process Tool)

Purpose
This process technique is used to facilitate the group and to help it move forward.

When to Use
Use this when the group needs a process intervention.

How to Use
Summarise the current situation or what is happening

> "I sense that there are a number of views around the table which all appear to be valid and we can't seem to agree on which one to tackle first"

Propose a way forward, a technique, or a model, which will help.

> "I propose that we use a Relative Importance Grid, list all issues and then all rate against each other".
> (Draw or write on a flip chart or hand-out Relative Importance Grids to illustrate what you are suggesting)

Outcome - give an idea of the intended outcome/output.

> "I think that this would enable us to see the issue(s) which are rated most significant by the majority and we would also see any that were felt strongly by a minority. We would then deal with them in order of significance."

Associated Process Tools

Symptom, Cause, Action (SCA)
Feedback Model (to check meaning of different options)
Going Dotty!
Essential and Desirable

Materials
Flip chart
Relative Importance Grid Forms
Paper
Marker pens

4. Four Box Model
(Data analysis)

Purpose
To structure the relationship between two aspects of a situation

When to Use
This model is useful when working with groups for plotting where 'things' fit when considered in relation to two different and possibly disparate descriptions.

How to Use
1.   Recognise that there is a relationship between two different parameters which are being discussed. This will be made clear from listening to the discussion/argument and 'hearing the process words' *not* focusing on the 'red' words.
2.   Test this relationship with the group by drawing two axes on the flip chart and suggesting what could be the titles along the horizontal axis and the vertical axis. Get the agreement of the group that the titles are appropriate for the situation (e.g. Skills and Market).
3.   Add four squares within the two axes and get the group to agree the description which relates to the extreme end of each axis (e.g. new : old). Write the descriptions, which you have agreed, onto the diagram and if necessary ask someone to feedback what the group has agreed.
4.   Agree with the group the question(s), which could be answered using this model. For instance :
   - if we are to grow the sales of our existing products which markets should we be targeting and can we do this with our existing skills ?
5.   Ask the members of the group to write on Post Its™ their descriptions of the various situations (e.g. the skills needed/not needed OR the new/old sector(s)).
6..   Ask people to put their post it(s)™ in the position, which is most appropriate (e.g. if they felt that moving into the (new) market would require new skills then they would place it in the top right hand square).
   Conversely, they might feel that selling into the new sector (another new market) could be achieved with existing skills – then it would be placed in the bottom right hand square.
7.   Continue until all situations have been identified and posted onto the model.

This technique can be modified for a wide range of situations. Some uses to date include

Situation	Axis titles	Extremes
Helping someone to identify their next career move	Sector : Skills	New : Old
Identifying the degree of empowerment of individuals	Control : Responsibility	High : Low
Recognising the causes of non achievement of individuals and departments	Challenge : Support	High : Low
Prioritising sales effort to realise the greatest financial return	Product : Potential Sales	Old : New High : Low
Identifying which teams to coach/support	Significance to the business: Level of Maturity	High: Low (Dys)Functional: Process Aware

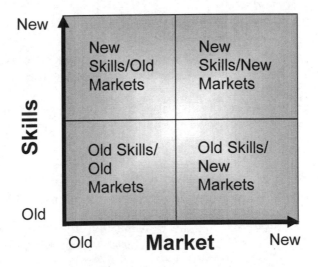

Materials
Flipchart
Post Its™
Coloured markers

Time
1 hour

Associated Process Tools
Feedback Model

5. Matrix Charting
(Data Analysis)

Purpose
This technique is used to help groups define or redefine organisational roles and responsibilities or as an aid to competency mapping.

When to Use
Matrix charting can be used when there are *three or more* categories of information or data in two dimensions (which in fact will be represented by the 'x' and 'y' axis – see examples in the diagrams below. This is different to the Four Box Model, which handles data on *two* dimensions but where there are only two points on each axis (e.g. 'high'/ 'low').

How to Use
Distribute a matrix to each group.

1. The group should be in a position where data and information is beginning to become too difficult to handle and deal with and where there are multiple dimensions across the 'x' and 'y' axis.

2. A skilled facilitator will be able to determine which Matrix is suitable for the Task:

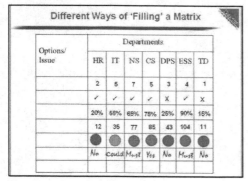

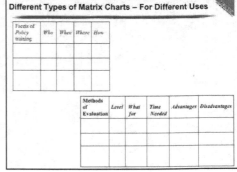

Diagram 1   Diagram 2

Diagram 1 contains all the different ways in which a Matrix can be populated:

- *Ranking or rating* - representing a 'position' relative to the other options. This would be appropriate if the group needed to 'rank' or determine the relative placing of each option *relative to the others.*

- *Yes or No* – this is used to represent that the option does or does not conform to a requirement. The group would use this if the options had to comply with a specific requirement.
- *Percentage Rating* – this would be used if you could give each option a percentage relative to the degree to which it fulfilled the criteria. The group would use this if they could give a rating to each option based on information.
- *Numbers* – this would be used if each option could be 'scored' and the scores add up to a total figure. The group would use this if each option was being 'scored' across different factors.
- *Traffic Lights* – used for visual effect to make a point that judgements could be made about each option – see below:
- *Yes, No, Maybe, Go, No Go, Possibly, Must, and Could,* – this is used to highlight potential of each option. The group would use this if a simple 'yes/no' was required or it was easy to make that 'call'.

Diagram 2 shows how the Matrix can contain descriptive words so that the group can gather and collate information about different proposals.

3. Ask the group to identify the data, which will go in the 'y' axis. This will usually be options, possibilities, Factors or issues (e.g. in problem solving). Then get the group to identify the columns on the 'x' axis and enter these across the matrix. Ideally, if the facilitator has acted quickly enough, the group will be able to fill the headings for the rows and the headings for the columns as they go along. This will avoid people trying to compare different rows and columns in their heads.

4. Once the 'x' column headings and 'y' axis row titles have been entered the group needs to offer the option of:
   - completing the matrix *horizontally* – each row at a time - comparing each column heading against each row option in sequence.
   - completing the matrix *vertically* – each column at a time - comparing each row option against each column heading in turn.
   The group also needs to be guided as to whether they undertake the data infilling as:
   - *All to One* – everyone contributes (out loud) and one person 'captures' their contributions and completes the matrix
   - *All* – each person completes a matrix himself or herself
   - *One to All* – One person fills in the matrix on behalf of everyone else (possibly after the meeting and presents it back next time)

> - *Group* – sub groups (representing different interest groups or mixed) can each work on the Matrix and compare their results afterwards.

5. Decide whether people tackle either *rows* or *columns*. In this way the task can be carried out 'in parallel. One person/group could do row 1, another row 2 etc. On the other hand, a person/group could do column 1 and another person/group column 2 etc.

Note: If one or more criteria is more important than another then if the group is using scores these can be 'weighted' (i.e. multiplied by a number – e.g. x 3)

Materials
Matrices
Flip chart
Markers

Time
One to one and a half hour

Associated Process Tools
Clustering
Feedback
Linking

6. Allegory - A Day at the Zoo
(Data collection)

Purpose
This type of imaginative technique is used to generate descriptions of:
* current situations
* how things should be
* two or more sets of circumstances relating to favourable and unfavourable situations

When to Use
It is best used in situations where people might have difficulty in describing the situation(s) or circumstances in real terms and, therefore, need to distance themselves from 'reality'. The best results are likely to be obtained when the technique is used in small groups.

How to Use
1. Explain to members of the group that you will be asking them to describe the situation under examination in terms of an allegory such as an animal (e.g. select the animal that best describes your department as it is now). The allegory used can be real, cartoon characters (e.g. Mickey Mouse), fictitious (e.g. Pegasus) or made up (e.g. a cross between a car and a dumper truck with huge wheels, small windscreen and no steering wheel!).

2. Using Post Its™ (one characteristic to one Post Its™) ask members of the group to list the characteristics of their chosen allegory to explain why they have chosen it to describe the 'now' features of the situation under review.

3. They should then put their Post Its™ on to the chart in column 1 (see diagram on page 139). No attempt should be made to cluster these characteristics because they are allegorical. However, the facilitator should encourage as much laughter and humour as possible. The reality of the situation will be encompassed in these characteristics and humour can defuse the tension.

4. Now ask people to work either, on their own (*All*) or in pairs/trios (depending on the size of the group) and to identify the *reality* associated with each Post Its™. So perhaps a small 'windscreen' means that the organisation cannot see where it is going (even though it is a huge organisation and can knock things out of its path –

'dumper truck'). These *real* characteristics should be placed in Column 2.

5. The facilitator should decide if everyone (*All*) will place their Post Its™ in column 2 and *then* cluster them or if one person at a time puts their (real) Post Its™ up (*One to All*) and others attach theirs to ones that are similar (e.g. windscreen – 'can't see where we are going' and blind mice – 'can't see'). Be conscious of the group dynamics – is there a tendency for one person to dominate or impose their view of the situation?

Now either:

6a. Ask members of the group to think of the situation under examination as they believe it *needs to be,* and again to describe it as an allegory and to write each characteristic on a separate Post Its™ and place them in column 3.

Or

6b. Get individual people working on individual clusters (from column 2) or people working in pairs/trios to identify *what the future (reality) situation should be like.* They should write the characteristics of the new reality on Post Its™ (remember a Post Its™ can be any size or shape as long as it has temporary glue backing – so don't restrict people to one word or short phrases when they need to write a description) and place them in column 4.

Or

6c Get one group to carry out the actions at 6a and another group to undertake the activities at 6b and combine the outputs.

7. If you have chosen 6a then, for each characteristic given, ask the group to explain what each one represents in the real situation (e.g. 'binoculars with good lenses' – meaning we can 'see ahead in great detail'). Again, be conscious of the group dynamics: is anyone seeking to impose their will; are some hanging back? Select the *format* (on page 12) appropriately. Whichever option you have chosen 6a, 6b or 6c then cluster the (reality) Post Its™ into meaningful clusters. Remember to encourage people to use the *Feedback Model as* they create each cluster to ensure that each contribution 'fits' that grouping. Avoid 'over-clustering' – some of the minority viewpoints might give the best clue to the future needs.

8. The clusters provide a number of potential options to change the current situation, which the group can examine in detail to trigger solutions and courses of action. If there are a number of potential options, you may want to suggest that the group select the most appropriate/useful ones. They can do this by using a Relative Importance Grid or Dots. Once the list has been refined to the Essential and Desirable then the group can begin creating an Action Plan (in column 5). This can be done using *Five Questions* as columns in the Action Plan (see Tool No: 13 on page 170).

Allegory - A Day at the Zoo

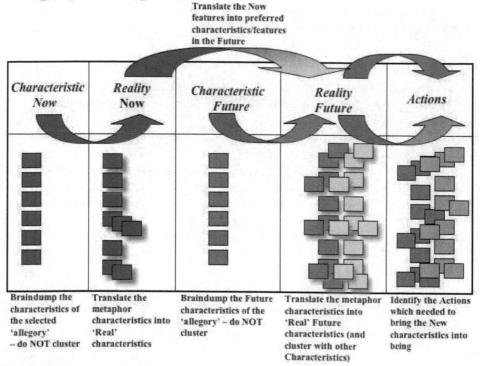

Translate the Now features into preferred characteristics/features in the Future

Characteristic Now	Reality Now	Characteristic Future	Reality Future	Actions
Braindump the characteristics of the selected 'allegory' – do NOT cluster	Translate the metaphor characteristics into 'Real' characteristics	Braindump the Future characteristics of the 'allegory' – do NOT cluster	Translate the metaphor characteristics into 'Real' Future characteristics (and cluster with other Characteristics)	Identify the Actions which needed to bring the New characteristics into being

Materials
Flip charts
Post It® Notes

Time
One to one and a half hours.

Associated Process Tools
Clustering and Linking
RIG and Dots
Five Questions **and** Force Field Analysis

7. Repertory Grid
(Data collection)

Purpose
To get the *common* factors, features or behaviours in a given situation compared with other situations.

When to Use
This technique is useful when people are finding it difficult to identify the factors, which are common in situations but hard to discern. For example, the factors, which help make a sale or the problems affecting a project or good leadership?

How to Use
1. Write out a description of the situation/problem being reviewed (e.g. 'what is causing us to do or not do well in interviews')

2. Get the individual(s) to think of up to six different examples of the situation (Elements). Invite them to choose specific occasions which were good/worked well and specific occasions when it went badly/did not work well. (e.g. 1. poor interview, 2. almost got the job, 3. did not do at all well, 4. nearly didn't but then did, 5. best interview, 6. worst interview). Write these into the column headings (A – H) on Form RG1 (see page 149). In general terms, the 'Elements' as they are called are derived from the following generic contexts:
   - Good
   - Bad
   - Worst
   - Best
   - Quite good
   - Quite bad
   - Could have been better
   - Could have been worse

These 'fit' most situations and can be adapted (see list further on).

TERM	DEFINITION
Element prompt	Description of the thing which people will use to identify examples from their own experience e.g. routine event/encouraging event; my boss/ good salesman
Element	Actual thing or event, which is focused on, when

	inviting a person to think about a situation. They can be people, situations or even events, which allow the constructs to be expressed.
Construct	Any similarity we have noted between events, which makes them different from other events. All constructs are bi-polar.
Bi-polar	By stating something IS we are also stating WHAT IT IS NOT. The extent of the bi-polar construct is a means of differentiating between people e.g. Honest ——————————— Dishonest Brave ——————————— Cowardly
Pole	Each construct discriminates between two poles, one at each end of the person's construing. The first is called the Similar Pole.
Similar Pole	Description which the person gives when identifying the similarity of two like elements.
Different Pole	Sometimes called opposite, this is the description given to the 'odd element' out.

3. You need to very clear about the question and to define it quite carefully (see Note at end). Ask the individual(s) to see if 'any two occasions/situations are similar' and to write the similarity down on a Post Its™ or on Form RG1 (see page 146). Get them to write positive similarities on one colour and negative similarities on another; one statement per post-it or the statement on one side of the Form and the 'opposite/difference' statement on the other side.

4. Take an answer (e.g. 'I didn't feel comfortable') and ask the person "what would I see happening in that situation?" Write their answers on smaller Post Its™. Ask the question again using their answer as the start point (e.g. 'They made me sit facing across a huge table'). Ask what the 'opposite (positive) is (e.g. 'We sat around a coffee table'). Keep asking the question this until the person 'grounds' their answer in the 'details'. Record the details on Form RG 2.

5. Take an answer and ask, "Why is that important to you?" (Only ask it of positive statements). Keep asking the question, using their previous answer until you get to their 'Values'. (e.g. "Why was it important for you to 'sit around a coffee table?" – 'It made me feel like we were equals'. "Why is it important for you to feel like 'we were equals'?" 'It makes me feel comfortable'). See technique, *What will I see happening …Why?* on page 153.

6. You can get the individual(s) to put their post its onto a flip chart as they go along, call out what they have found or do it in silence and collect their Post Its™. The format will depend on whether you want to avoid duplication, to stimulate ideas or ensure non-interference of people's thought processes.

   a. Cluster the ideas with positive on one side and negative on the other. See if there are opposites. Where there is not, put up the 'opposite'.

   b. Alternatively, you can get the individuals to 'score' their Form RG1s. They should follow the instructions at the bottom of Form RG1. You need to make sure that they also complete the 'imposed construct' scoring. This will be used as a benchmark to identify which 'constructs' are the most significant.

   c. After everyone has completed their Form, reverse the scores for their imposed construct at the bottom of the Form (as shown on the example of the Form on page 147). Compare the scores against each *construct* with the *'imposed'* construct (as shown for Construct 1 – the numbers *above* the original score). Then re-score using the reversed imposed construct (the numbers *below* the original scores). Add these scores up across the row and put the totals in the far column (see example for row/Construct 1). Then take one score away from the other and the 'Total' is the 'weight' or significance of that construct. The smallest number indicates whether it is the *left hand side* of the construct or the *right hand* side, which is the 'preferred statement/construct. The larger the number the more significant that construct. Score the whole grid and this will identify the key constructs.

   d. Use the list to examine the situation and to work on action planning.

What Counts as an Effective Element

The success of any Repertory Grid based project is based on the appropriateness of the Elements.

Elements should represent the topic 'evenly'. For instance, in order to identify the characteristics of Managers in your organisation you could ask your interviewees to select a range of managers for comparison.

e.g. a good manager, a poor manager, a new manager, an old manager, a manager I would like to work for, a manager I would not like to work for, the best manager I have ever worked for (in this organisation or another)

Nouns make good elements; the more concrete the noun the better. You may decide that you would like to use situations as Elements. It is important to make sure that your interviewees identify and focus on specific situations which fit each element prompt during the course of their interview.

For example, situations like: organising a Sales Conference: presenting the departmental objectives to the Board and participating in the project team, which introduced product X.

Do not mix verbs with nouns or very abstract ideas with very concrete ones. Try to avoid using, as elements things which are really constructs. How can you tell? Any word with an easy opposite is likely by definition to be a construct.

Constructs
The phrase which expresses 'what the two elements have in common' is called the Similar Pole and the phrase that characterises the 'odd one out' is called the Different pole). The purpose of construct elicitation is to express the whole construct: that is, both poles. This is because the meaning of the term depends on its difference/opposite.

To say that a person has 'well developed judgement' as opposed to being 'foolish' is to express a very different meaning from saying has 'well developed judgement' as opposed to 'being of low intelligence.

Beware of the logical opposite! In other words, do not assume or accept as a different pole the word use for the similar pole with a prefix such as 'not', 'un' or its grammatical equivalent. 'Has well developed judgement – Hasn't got well developed judgement' would have obscured the meaning more fully expressed in the previous example. When the person offers you, a different pole, which is just the logical opposite, ask the question 'in what way the opposite'.

Identifying Element Prompts
Elements are the 'things' from which a person can construe. They can be people, situations or events that allow constructs to be expressed. Some suggested element prompts are:
A project which went well,
A project which did not go well,
A project which started well but then went badly
A project which started badly and got better
the best project I have even been involved in.
OR

A manager who motivated me,
A manager who did not motivate me,
A person I would like to work for
A manager I would like to work for
the best 'motivator' I have ever worked for.
OR
A specific task/job I enjoy doing
A specific task/job I do not enjoy doing
A specific task/job I would like the opportunity to do again
A specific task/job I do not want to do again – ever
A specific task/job I keep for myself
A specific task/job I want to 'get rid of'
OR
A product I enjoy working on
A product I do not enjoy working on
A product would not ever like to work on
A product I would love to work on
A product I have worked on in the past
OR
A time I felt motivated
A time I found that, I was de-motivated
A time I was motivated and then became de-motivated
A time I wasn't initially motivated but became demotivated
The time I have been the most motivated in my life
The time I have been the most de-motivated in my life

Identify the 'question'
The process requires that people make comparisons between the elements which they have identified from their own experience and which fit the descriptions of the element prompts. In order that valuable constructs can be elicited from these comparisons, it is necessary for people to have a context in which to consider the things that they are comparing.

For example, the question will be one or a combination of the following:

"How are two similar and different from the third in the way in which..."
The wider the question, the scope of the constructs will be broader. The narrow the question, the more defined the construing.
For example, 'How are two cars similar in the way they drive?' will elicit narrower constructs than 'How are two cars similar?'
For more information, a more detailed explanation of Repertory Grid or a manual please contact: tony.mann@resourcestrategicchange.com

Materials
Flip chart
Post Its™ (two different colours)
Felt pens
Blank RG1 and RG2 Forms

Time
Up to 75 minutes to get clusters

Associated Process Tools
Linking
Five Questions
What will I see happening…Why?

Key Process Models, Tools and Techniques

FORM: RG1
Constructs
Initials of Interviewer:

DATA COLLECTION

Name of interviewee: John Smithson
Tel No (for reference):..................

No	Construct	A	B	C	D	E	F	G	H	Construct	Score
1	The 'panel' gave me time to answer	1	3	4	2	3	2	4	4	I was rushed into giving my opinion	
2	I was sat opposite them and they sat behind a large table	4	3	2	4	1	5	3	2	We were sat around a coffee table	
3	I had read up about the company and knew what they did	1	3	4	1	4	1	3	4	I couldn't get much information beforehand	
4	They asked questions which seemed ambiguous	4	3	2	4	3	4	3	1	The questions were straightforward	
5											
	Imposed Construct (Positive) *The best interview I have had*	2	3	5	1	4	2	3	5	Imposed Construct (Negative) *The worst interview I have had*	
	For interviewer's use only	4	3	1	5	2	4	3	1		

SCORING :. Reverse the scores for their imposed construct at the bottom of the Form

The Art, Science and Skill of Facilitation

FORM: RG1
Constructs
Initials of Interviewer:

DATA COLLECTION

Name of interviewee: John Smithson
Tel No (for reference): ....

No	Construct	A	B	C	D	E	F	G	H	Construct	Score
1	The 'panel' gave me time to answer	1	0	1	1	1	0	1	1	I was rushed into giving my opinion	6
		1	3	4	2	3	2	4	4		10L
		3	0	3	3	1	2	1	3		16
2	I was sat opposite them and they sat behind a large table	4	3	2	4	1	5	3	2	We were sat around a coffee table	
3	I had read up about the company and knew what they did	1	3	4	1	4	1	3	4	I couldn't get much information beforehand	
4	They asked questions which seemed ambiguous	4	3	2	4	3	4	3	1	The questions were straightforward	
5											
	Imposed Construct (Positive) *The best interview I have had*	2	3	5	1	4	2	3	5	Imposed Construct (Negative) *The worst interview I have had*	
	For interviewer's use only	4	3	1	5	2	4	3	1		

SCORING :. Reverse the scores for their imposed construct at the bottom of the Form (as shown in blue). Compare the scores against each construct with the 'imposed' construct (as shown for Construct 1 – the top scores in light blue). Then re-score using the reversed imposed construct (the bottom scores in brown). Add these scores up across the row and put the total in the far right column (see example for row/Construct 1). Then take one score away from the other and the 'Total' is the 'weight' or significance of that construct. The smallest number indicates whether it is the *left hand side* of the construct or the *right hand* side which is the 'preferred statement/construct. The larger the number the more significant that construct. Score the whole grid and this will identify the key constructs.

Key Process Models, Tools and Techniques

Evidence Statements

FORM RG2

Construct No	Evidence	Value

Initials of Interviewer:

The Art, Science and Skill of Facilitation

DATA COLLECTION

Name of Interviewee:

Tel No (for reference): ....

Grp	No	Construct	A	B	C	D	E	F	G	H				Construct
	1													
	2													
	3													
	4													
	5													
	6													
	7													
	8													
		Imposed Construct (Positive)												Imposed Construct (Negative)

SCORING : If the person/situation you are scoring is most like the statement on the left then put a '1' in the square. If the person/situation you are scoring is most like the statement on the right then put a '5' in the square. If neither of these extreme scores applies then use 2, 3 and 4 as appropriate. **Please fax the completed sheet to:**

149

8. Restatement/Provocation
(Data collection)

Purpose
This technique enables groups to gain a new perception on a particular problem or situation.

When to Use
Restatement/Provocation can be used when groups are bogged down in a particular approach to a problem. When they "can't see the wood for the trees".

Early in the process of developing a watershed plan or non-point source management plan, how problems get defined can have a major impact on everything that follows. Problems that are too vague or too narrowly defined can result in projects with vague goals or solutions that fail to address the source of the problem.

A common pitfall in problem definition is confusing problems and solutions. An example of a solution stated as a problem is, "We don't have enough riparian buffers on our headwater streams". By defining the problem as "lack of riparian buffers", you limit the options for solving the problem to only one: increasing riparian buffers. If, on the other hand you define the problem as "excess nutrients entering the stream", this broader definition allows consideration of any alternative that will prevent nutrients from entering the stream.

One reason we confuse solutions with problems is that we make assumptions about the problem. When we question our assumptions about a problem, we often find that we need to broaden our definition of the problem. In the above example, if we assume that excess nutrients are caused by surface runoff of fertilizers from farm fields, we might mistakenly define the problem as a lack of riparian buffers. However, if we question our assumption about the source of the nutrients, we might discover that most of the farm fields are drained by sub-surface tiles, which bypass riparian buffers. So, if we define the problem as insufficient buffers, we might fail to address the problem of excess nutrients.

Example:
In a similar situation, members of a Tennis Club were upset that non-paying members were using the courts. All kinds of suggestions were put forward as to how to deal with the problem. The Club Secretary was requested to ask people for their membership cards. This did not work because people did not carry their membership cards. Gates were

padlocked and the keys issued prior to games but people left the gates open, so that idea failed. Some months later, the Committee met again. This time someone asked if they could re-assess the question and after numerous attempts it was suggested that the real question was "how to recognise Members without being able to recognise them personally". After some laughter and people dismissing this as silly and obvious, the group realised that *if* you could recognise a member *from* a non-member, then you would know instantly who was legitimate. Then someone used an analogy of how do farmers know their sheep or cows from a distance and someone said "by their branding or markings". Someone then said, "How can we 'brand' our members?" After some laughter, another person said that "brands stayed on regardless and the sheep couldn't take them off". More laughter as it was suggested that members be branded (just as if they are in a nightclub!). This Committee Chair was not amused until someone said, "What if members were given a 'token' which went through the laces of their tennis shoes, wouldn't that distinguish them from non-members and as people usually wore the same shoes wouldn't that be a sort of 'brand'?" Everyone thought and suddenly they realised it was the answer to: "how to recognise Members without being able to recognise them personally". It became the responsibility of *everyone* to check on people playing and it was easy. Non-members soon realised that they could not just turn up and it even resulted in people paying their annual subscription on time, because the colour of the token changed every year and it was embarrassing to have last year's colour!

How to Use
1. Write up a description of the situation or problem for everyone to see and put up a piece of flip chart paper for new ideas.

2. Simplify the description, eradicating any hint at solutions or causes and write a simple statement of the situation.

3. Underline the key words.

4. Encourage people to think of the opposite of the key words or generate words, which mean something very different from the key words in the context of the statement of the situation (e.g. Members – non-members, public, terrorists, cinema goers).

5. As a new word is generated construct a new statement by putting it in one of the previous statements or the original statement, as appropriate. Mix and match at will.

6. Record the outputs on the flip chart paper. Do not evaluate or judge at this stage, this will require the use of another technique. Use frequent feedback and summary to ensure that everyone understands each new statement as it is generated.

7. Encourage the use of analogies (see page 123).

8. Look again at the problem or situation to see if there is another/new perspective.

Materials

Flip chart
Markers of different colours
Post Its™

Time
30 minutes

Associated Process Tools
Analogy

9. What will I see happening …...Why?
(Data collection)

Purpose
This technique enables us to focus on an issue and to become more and more specific, to make sure that what is being addressed is important and to identify the values which drive that behaviour or action.

When to Use
The technique is most useful when there is a problem or situation that appears very vague. More focus and detail is required so that the real issues can be addressed. It is also useful when trying to elicit the rationale for beliefs, actions and behaviours.

How to Use
1. Get a description of the problem/situation written up on a flip chart. Ask 'What will I have seen happening in this situation/problem?' You are looking to get the FACTS. For example:
   Descriptive statement: 'The manufacturer's fault was not put right during the service and the customer complained.'

2. Write up the statement(s) made on Post Its® and put them underneath the description *on the left hand side*. Ask again '(so) what will I have seen happening …?' For example:
   Fact statement: 'We didn't record which cars needed the fault repair and which did not.'
   Again, record this on a Post Its™ and put *on the left hand side.*

3. Ask 'What prevented you/stopped you/hindered you *recording which cars needed the fault repair*?' You are looking for reasons rather than mere facts. So for example:
   Reason: 'There is no field on the computer screen to enter an item such as 'manufacturer's faults.'
   Record this reason on a different colour Post Its® and put it *opposite* the fact.

4. Keep asking 'What will I have seen/see happening?' until you have all the key facts and reasons for them happening. You could ask 'What do you mean by *field on the screen?*' which might explain what the person means by 'field'. So for example:
   Meaning: 'A place where we are allowed to enter data, using our password'.

Pyramiding	A questioning technique which elicits factual information (on behaviour) and identifies more concrete less attitudinal information. Ask 'What …?' 'How ...?' (e.g. 'What would I see that person doing?')
Platforming	A questioning technique about meanings to give greater understanding to what is being said. This allows the analyst to compare data more accurately. Ask 'What do you mean by that … (word/phrase/ statement)..?'

You can 'Pyramid up and down the positive (+ve) and the negative (–ve) 'poles' between *Characteristics* and *Behaviours/Features*. However, you can only 'Ladder' up the +ve pole to *Values*. Do not attempt to identify Negative (–ve) Values!

Laddering	A questioning technique which elicits values, ethics and identifies higher-level information. This is personal to the respondent and drives their behaviour and actions. Ask 'Why…is that important to you...?'

Therefore, the process looks like an 'h' – see diagram on the next page. Diagram 1 illustrates the process. Diagram 2 illustrates the completed exercise with data.

The Art, Science and Skill of Facilitation

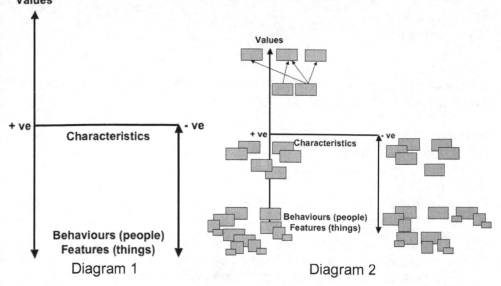

Diagram 1

Diagram 2

Materials
Flip chart
Pens
Post Its® of different colours
Felt tipped pens

Time
Approximately 45 minutes

Associated Process Tools
Five Questions
Force Field Analysis
Storytelling
Allegory – A Day at the Zoo

For more information, a more detailed explanation of Repertory Grid or a manual please contact: tony.mann@resourcestrategicchange.com

10. Storytelling
(Data collection)

Purpose:
To describe a personal or organisational 'history' and future in a way which gives it a sense of interest and feeling?

When to use:
When the actual details might be too unpalatable or difficult to accept 'head-on', or where it would be interesting to describe something in an unusual way.

Principles (taken from the experience of the Department of Trade and Industry in the UK):

a. *relevance*: story-telling puts learning into context through examples that demonstrate outcomes (e.g. "one thing that made a difference was the team being briefed all together". "It occurred once when ..."). Knowledge plus context plus benefits equals greater relevance and therefore a greater probability of effective learning.

b. *flexibility:* story-telling provides some key learning points, but preserves flexibility around their application. The lack of structure to a process and the impact of unique factors suggests that any manual attempting to set out how to do it would be re-written each time the process of repeated. The story-telling approach avoids this dead end.

c. *richness:* stories have the potential to transfer both tacit and codified knowledge, being much more likely to convey the subtle understandings which would rarely survive information gathered via a questionnaire or disseminated via a procedure manual.

d. *transferability:* story-telling is a natural form of human communication. If the stories are good (particularly if they fit the culture), they will spread by word of mouth with little further effort, and will hang around for longer in the corporate memory.

How to use:
Method One

1. Break the group into sub groups of four people (A, B, C, and D). Ask person 'A' and 'C' to tell persons 'B' and 'D' the facts about the situation.

Round One

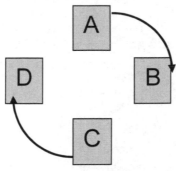

2. Ask persons 'B' and 'D' to tell persons 'A' and 'C' the story that they have just been told. This time they should simplify it and embellish the main points (as they see them).

Round Two

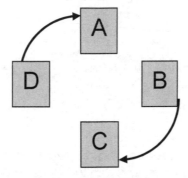

3. This time person 'A' and 'C' retell the facts as an allegorical story, making up characters, plots, and background to make the facts more interesting.

Round Three

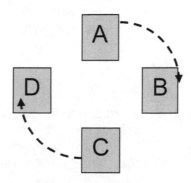

4. In the fourth round, the storytellers embellish the story adding detail and emphasis and character(s). They can turn the story into the opposite of the original and emphasis the positive rather than the negative. It will now be told to the person who originally shared the bare facts. They should judge whether the 'story' is a true reflection of the facts and whether it captures the essence of the tale.

Round Four

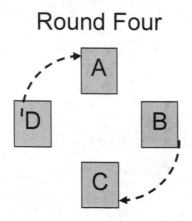

The story may then be written down, captured as a narrative, and retold whenever appropriate. Below is the gist of an actual story that was created by a change agent in a large company to illustrate the change team's strength in terms of their credibility in the face of them beginning to have self-doubt.

'The King was in a foul mood, he summoned the head of his army and said "I know that your men fight very hard and have won great battles but the King's coffers are low, it had been hard to raise Taxes and we need to use our money wisely. I will need you to make savings and to use your weapons for longer and to repair your chariots, rather than get new ones. However, I do expect you to take the Land of Cazoon and to win the land for us in the forthcoming battle. Your men must fight harder and more bravely than ever before. The head of the army left feeling very dejected. Just at that moment a cry went up from outside the Palace..
"He's coming ...he's coming".
"Who's coming shouted the King".
"The Giant said the King's minister".
"Fetch Merlin then" shouted the King
Merlin was fetched and arrived before the King to be told of the great calamity that the dreaded giant from the other side of the mountain was coming at last to their land. Merlin had fought and killed dragons and seen off many a witch but this giant had a different reputation. Merlin

secretly doubted his powers to fight and kill the giant who had defeated many a magician in other lands. He was about to tell the King that perhaps he should send the army or that the King would have to send him on a giant killing course (!) when his young sorcerer drew Merlin aside and whispered to him. Merlin listened and instead told the King:
"I will do my duty my Lord and deal with the troublesome giant". The King was relieved for Merlin had always served him well and had always been there to save the Kingdom, no matter how large the dragon.
With that, Merlin set off and called all the wizards from across the land and swearing them to secrecy he ordered them to read the ancient books and work on new spells. Finally, Merlin learnt the secret of how to defeat the giant and came back to the King. By now, the giant was nearing the Palace having caused mayhem across the Kingdom. The army had failed to halt his progress and had withdrawn to sharpen their damaged swords.
Merlin stepped out of the Palace gates and walked towards the giant before the giant could get near enough to trouble the King, who was hiding in the back of the Palace. Merlin used his new found powers and with one mighty spell the giant was bound and helpless and screamed to be let go promising he would never come back again. At which point Merlin called the army who lifted the giant onto their rickety carts and trundled him away to the border.
The King was elated and showered honours on Merlin. So what had the sorcerer said to Merlin that eventful day? He had reminded Merlin that not only was he a magician but he was revered and that his reputation lay in the fact that no one knew what or how he did what he did. They just knew that he could. He told Merlin not to reveal his fear or his doubts but to find the solution. The King wouldn't care how Merlin did it as long as he did.'

This story reminded the change management team of the awe in which they were held and that they need not seek approval for the training and outside help they sought, as long as they achieved what they always did. They should not seek funding or training but rather do what they needed to do to give themselves the skills they needed, because the 'King' relied on them and held them in great respect. The team applauded this storyteller and they set about writing their *own* development plan without fear of funding or time constraints. Knowing that it was outcomes not inputs that would be measured – unlike the Sales Force who were being cut back and yet had to make more sales and achieve more market position than ever before!

Method Two:
Turning the situation (as it is) into a story

1. Invite people to think about the situation and then imagine it in an allegorical sense. Encourage them to think of it in terms of a 'fairytale' a cartoon a drama or anything which takes it into a 'fantasy'. They may need some help to do this, so, encourage them to work in pairs and to tell their partner the basic outline and encourage the other person to 'translate' it into another 'arena'. Usually, with a little encouragement, people can find an alternative 'vehicle' for their story.

2. Then get people to draw on small cards or straight onto a sheet of A3 paper the gist of their story. This can either be in words or in pictures, like the storyboard for a film (see blank storytelling 'framework' at the end of this technique).

3. Then invite them to move the cards or the sentences around till they make sense and capture the essence of the story. Some facts may be discarded at this point or others introduced.

4. Now, encourage them to make up a short two-minute story to explain the situation. They should tell this short story to their partner.

5. After the telling they, and the other person, will think of other things which can go into the story to embellish it and make it more interesting and exciting.

Writing the future

6. The storyteller should now look forward and add the future into their story building in characters and storylines which tell the story as it *will be in the future* (hopefully). The storyteller now builds their story into a fuller version which may be anything from four minutes to ten, if the story has a lot of elements.

7. Now, the storyteller tells the full story, with the *past* and *future* elements built in, to the other person or the whole group.

8. The story can be recorded by hand, in a computer or by audio/video means.

Applying the story
Invite people to:

- talk in trios about their favourite part of the story and what they think the main lessons about the situation are.

- try and identify the particular turning points during the story: how did they happen, who did what and what effect did it have? What does that mean in practice?

- think about different ways of dealing with some of the problems described in the story.

- think about the implications for the future and what needs to be done to make the story happen. Write the actions on Post Its™ and have them ready to share.

If this sort of approach works and you want to take things further, you could also:-

- retell the story from the perspective of different participants

- retell the story, distorting it so that it is much better (a perfect journey) or worse (a nightmare journey) than it is told in the original.

You may want to hand out *Tips for Storytelling* (on the next page).

Materials:
Wide variety of coloured post-its
Coloured felt tip pens
A4 paper
Audio/video recorder
Computer

Time:
This is hugely variable. 30 minutes for a simple story and up to 2 hours to build a complex story covering difficult issues.

Useful Sites:
http://www.scottishstorytellingcentre.co.uk/
http://www.sfs.org.uk/

Tips for storytelling

Storytellers learn their stories in many different ways. Some read or listen to a story over and over. Some meditate on it. Some type or write out the story. Some draw charts. Some begin telling the story at once.

Some parts of the story can be memorized word for word—beautiful beginnings and endings, important dialogue, colorful expressions, rhymes and repeated phrases. But *don't* try to memorize the entire story that way. Strict reciting makes it into a presentation which lacks warmth and feeling. Instead, *picture* the story. See the scenes in your mind, as clearly as you can. Later, these pictures will help you recreate your story as you tell it—whether you consciously call them to mind or not.

First, practice getting the storyline. Your version won't convey everything from the story you found, but it must convey enough to make sense. Then, once the story is straight in your mind, focus on *how* you tell it.

Use repetition. Pay special attention to repeated rhymes and phrases. Repetition helps your listeners stick with the story by providing familiar landmarks.

Alongside repetition, use variety. Vary the tone, pitch, and volume of your voice, your speed, your rhythms, and your articulation (smooth or sharp). Use silences. Remember, variety catches and holds attention.

Use gestures, but only ones that help the story. Use them to mime the action, or just for emphasis. Make them big! Gestures keep the eyes on *you.*

In your story, pay special attention to beginnings and endings. You may want to practice an introduction along with the story. This introduction can tell something about the story or about you. But don't give away the plot!

Endings should be clear, so your listeners know that your story's over without your telling them. You can do this by slowing down and adding emphasis. For example, many story endings use a "slow three"—"*happily ever after*," "*that's* the *end* of *that*," "and they *never saw him again.*"

Also pay special attention to how you portray your characters. Good characters bring a story to life—so put life into them, with face, voice, gesture and body posture. Try to make each of them different enough so they're easily told apart.

When portraying two characters talking together, try a trick called "cross-focus": Make each one face a different 45-degree angle.

You'll tell stories at your best if you prepare, not only your story, but, yourself. Your voice and body are your instruments, and it helps to use them well.

162

To project and sustain your voice, you must breathe deeply and correctly. To check this, place your hand on your stomach. As you inhale and your lungs expand, you should feel your stomach *push out.* Many people do the opposite, holding in their stomachs and breathing only with their upper chests. Also be sure to keep your back straight, so your lungs can expand fully.

Don't push your voice too hard or use it unnaturally (except maybe when speaking as a character.) To avoid strain, relax your throat and jaw muscles and the rest of your body as well. A big, loud sigh will help this. Also try the "lion's yawn"—open your mouth wide and stick your tongue out as far as it goes.

Pronounce each sound of each word distinctly. Tongue twisters are good for making the tongue more nimble.

Storytelling – Creating a story - Storyboard
Steps
Step 1:
Think about the situation and the characteristics of that situation, the way things operate, the way the company works and the people in it.

Step 2:
When you have some idea of what the situation 'looks like' and feels like think about what that reminds you of – does it sound like an orchestra with different musicians playing different pieces? Or, maybe an ant colony, working away for some purpose which is not readily obvious? Or a bus – going somewhere along predictable routes? Or two sides in a battle? Are their enemies outside? Does the orchestra have competition for funds? Is it difficult to play the music because of distractions? Is the ant colony always being disturbed? You use whatever analogy fits for you.

Step 3:
Create a story around this current state of affairs. Take a page and think about it as a storyboard. Write an aspect in each 'square'.

Take as many squares as you need to tell your story.

Step 4:
Now, think about what you *would like the situation in which the company operates to be like* **in the future.**
Re-tell the story as it would be in the future. Perhaps the orchestra has the music and a conductor and the auditorium is better?

Step 5:
Now practice telling your story as a script, adding any embellishments you like – e.g. "the orchestra plays lots of different types of music and the

audiences always applaud loudly". "The bus has a new route and in fact goes to different places everyday".

Say your story aloud and keep adding 'bits' as you think about it. Practice it but do not over-tell it, keep it fresh.

Write any notes to remind you how to tell it and bring your story to the event.

11. Is and Is Not
(Data collection/analysis)

Purpose
The search for the cause of a problem is narrowed down to a search for a change which could produce the effects, observed through some area of distinction

When to Use
When it is important to identify what the problem *IS NOT* in order to narrow down to what it might be.

How to Use
1. Agree and display a description of the situation. Do not worry about trying to define the cause or the actual cause of the problem.

2. Have someone act as scribe either using a flip chart or Post Its™. Get that person to ask the group the following types of questions.

- What distinguishes the situation?
- Where is the distinction?
- When is there a distinction?
- Who is the distinction?
- How much is the situation different?

For example:
'the overseas market is profitable – the home market is not'
'the xxx product is selling well – the yyy product is selling poorly'
'the best sales are in June/July – the best sales are not in the October/November'
'the European Sales team make a profit – the South East Asia team do not'
'the best sales are $z – the worst sales are $w'

3. This data should be recorded on a table such as the one on the next page.

4. When the group has identified the *Is* and *Is Not* then they can begin to identify what is distinctive about the Is/Is Not statements.

	Is	Is Not	What is Distinctive?	Any significance in this?
What : Object				
Where :				
When :				
Who:				
Extent/How much				

When the group has identified the *Is* and *Is* Not they can then begin to identify what is distinctive about the *Is/Is Not* statements.

Note: Remember that 'Where' can be *geographical* or *structural/organisational.* 'When' can be defined in years; seasons; months; weeks; days; hours and minutes!

A worked example of how to use the *Is and Is Not* tool is contained in the *Facilitation – a Handbook of Models, Tools and Techniques for Effective Group work* written by the same author[14].

Materials
Flip chart
Post Its™
Marker pens

Time
Up to 60 minutes to complete all stages unless additional information is needed to answer the *Is* and *Is Not* statements

Associated Process Tools
Clustering
Linking
Five Questions

For more detailed information on problem solving techniques and approaches visit: http://www.kepner-tregoe.com/

---

[14] ISBN 978-0-9556435-1-4

12. Debate
(Decision Making)

Purpose
This process technique is used to help the group make important decisions where 'voting' would be inappropriate.

When to Use
Use when the group needs to reach consensus and agreement.

How to Use
1.   The issue/options are displayed on the flip chart and individuals are asked to say what the option(s) are (but not at this stage to make a 'case' for them). Others give their interpretation and the Facilitator revises/adapts/alters/amends the statement(s) until there is agreement about the option(s).
2.   The Facilitator then asks everyone to write on Post Its™ points in favour of each option and points/issues against it (using the most appropriate format). These Post Its™ are displayed against each option.
3.   The Facilitator invites individuals to 'sponsor' each of the options and people to support them. As an alternative, the Task Leader could nominate people or people who 'oppose' an option could be asked to join one each of the 'sponsors'.
4.   The sponsor and their 'team' then work on presenting the option in the most effective way (using something like an SPO format).
5.   Each team then presents their option one at a time. The rest of the group is asked firstly to give Feedback on what they are hearing the sponsor say. Then to ask questions as required clarifying issues.
6.   The Facilitator then asks everyone to write on Post Its™ again points in favour of each option and points/issues against it. These are posted against each option.
7.   The sponsor and their co-presenters then review the Post Its™, cluster them into themes and prepare to address the issues raised.
8.   Each sponsor then addresses the group and counters the arguments.
9.   The Task Leader then asks anyone to propose which option the group should accept. They then ask the whole group for support for this proposal or counter proposals.
10. This should whittle the options down in number and the process of: sponsoring; writing Post Its™; addressing the issues and proposing continues until a clear option emerges.

Materials
Flip chart
Post Its™
Marker pens

Time
As required

Associated Process Tools
Feedback Model (to check meaning of different options)
Braindumping and Clustering
Force Field
Five Questions

13. Five Questions
(Data collection and Implementation)

Purpose
This technique is used to help groups and individuals to analyse problems, to develop solutions and to create action plans.

When to Use
Five questions is used to best effect in circumstances which require a logical and reasoned approach to problem solving and implementation.

How to Use
Create a chart to record the groups' findings and a table to record individuals' responses.

Problem Analysis
1. Ask the group to answer the following basic questions relating to the problem situation:
    *   basic questions:
        - what is done?
        - where is it done?
        - when is it done?
        - who does it?
        - how is it done?

These questions are answered from the factual information held by members of the group.
Record the results and display for all to see.

Rationale
2. Ask the following to justify the answers given to the basic questions:
    *   justification:
        - why is it done?
        - why there?
        - why then?
        - why by that person?
        - why in that way?

This identifies the rationale behind issues and elicits false values (see' *What will I see Happening....Why?* - page 153)

Solution Finding
3. Follow up with questions to get the group to consider alternatives and options:
    *   alternative questions:

- what else could be done?
- where else could it be done?
- when else could it be done?
- who else could do it?
- how else could it be done?

These questions and those in 4 below form the basis for the development of new methods and procedures. Record the results.

Refining
4. Ask the group to build and refine on the responses given above by asking them the following questions:
    *   subsidiary questions:
        - what should be done?
        - where should it be done?
        - when should it be done?
        - who should do it?
        - how should it be done?

This begins to shape the future state and to consolidate new ideas and Approaches.

Action Planning
5. In order to ensure that the implementation is effective ask the five questions about each action point in turn:
        - what do we need to do?
        - where do we need to do it?
        - when do we do it?
        - who could do it?
        - how could we do it?

6. In order to fully develop the new ideas it might well be necessary to use some of the more open process tools like *Braindumping*, (from *Facilitation – a Handbook of Models, Tools and Techniques for Effective Group Working*), *Allegory, Storytelling* and *even Force Field Analysis* – page 173.

Stage	What?	Where?	When?	Who?	How?
Problem Analysis					

Solution Finding				
Refining				
Action Panning/ Implementation				

Materials
Checklist of questions
Flip chart
Markers
Chart to record findings

Time
An hour and a half to two hours

Associated Process Tools
Is and Is Not
Linking
Clustering
Relative Importance Grid/Dots
Essential and Desirable
Storytelling
Allegory
Force Field Analysis

14. Force Field Analysis
(Implementation)

Purpose
This technique is used to identify and emphasise the relevance and significance of the forces that help and hinder a change, problem, situation or solution.

When to Use
The technique is most useful when assessing the ease of difficulty or achieving a particular course of action. It assists with planning to remove barriers and in assessing the relative strength of contributory causes of a particular problem.

How to Use
1. Agree and display the situation as it is.
2. Agree and display the situation, as the group wants it to be. You might want to use *Allegory – A Day at the Zoo* (page 137) or *Storytelling* (156) to identify the 'new' state.

3. Using Braindumping, Expert Witness or other data collection methods[15] to identify all the forces (positive and negative) that would impact on making the change from 'what it is' to 'what you want it to be' and write them on two different colours of Post Its™. You will need to think about what *format* to use *All; All to One; One to All* or *Group* (page 12). Which one you choose will depend on the group dynamics. Whether you need to hold certain people in check or bring people out.

4. Place them on a Force Field Diagram (see below).

Forces For +											Forces Against -									
10	9	8	7	6	5	4	3	2	1	0	1	2	3	4	5	6	7	8	9	10

[15] *Facilitation – a Handbook of Models, Tools and Techniques for Effective Group:* ISBN 978-0-9556435-1-4

Take note of the group dynamics: are people holding back (use *Group*); is someone potentially going to dominate (use *All*).

Impact:
- not significant   1
- medium significance   5
- major significance   10

5. If you are using the advanced Force Field Form (see below) then define rating scales for Ease of Change and Impact. For example, if the scales were 1 to 10, then scores would be gauged as follows:

Hard to Change
- cannot be changed   1
- could be changed   5
- can be changed easily   10

Can be Re-inforced
- Easily   10
- Possibly with some effort   5
- Hard to re-inforce   1

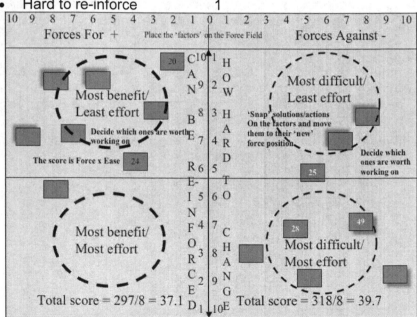

6. In terms of the following, evaluate each of the forces identified:
- ease of change (how far it is possible to reduce 'power' of this negative force)
- ease of re-inforcement (how easy it is to re-inforce this positive force)

- impact (how significant the consequences of changing the force would be)

and place them on the Force Field 'map'. Take account of the group dynamics. If there is someone likely to impose their view, then consider using a *Group* format.

7. Calculate the scores for each force (Impact vs Change/Re-inforce) recording the results on each Post Its™. This will give an overall assessment of the strength of the Forces For and Against. It may even help the group to see whether the strategy/plan/proposal has any hope of being implemented.

8. Given that the group considers that the Forces For outweigh the Forces Against or that there is the potential to challenge the Forces Against identify the issues which might have the potential to change. You could do these using different formats: *All; All to One; One to All* or *Group.* If you are using *Group* or *All, then* you may chose to use Dots to identify which forces people feel would be the key ones to tackle.

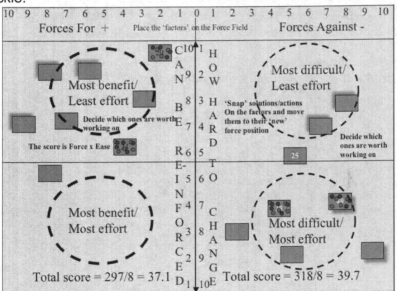

9. Once the group has selected the most significant Forces to work on they should 'Snap' ideas/solutions on to the issues and see what impact this has on the force. Does it make it less significant (-ve forces) or more powerful (+ve forces). Has it increased its effect (+ve) or reduced its power (-ve). Re-evaluate the 'scores' and assess whether overall the force for the plan/proposal/policy/strategy is greater than that against. Keep doing this until the group feels that they understand the situation and feel in control.

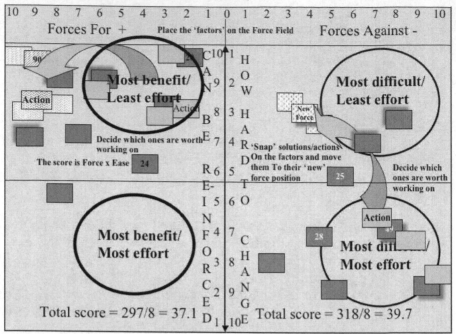

10. The Group should then be in a position to put together an Action Plan (using *Five Questions* – page 170).

The group can use 'backdrops' to their Force Fields as shown below with for example the Process Iceberg® - see page 172)

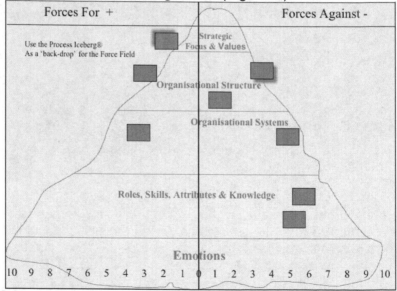

Materials

Force Field Diagram drawn large on several sheets of paper on a wall
Markers of different colours and thicknesses

Flip chart paper
Post Its™

Time
1 to 2 hours

Associated Process Tools
Brain Dumping
Clustering
Data collection methods
Relative Importance Grid
Dots
Five Questions

15. Process Review Iceberg® Model
(Process Model)

Purpose
The Process Iceberg® Review model is designed to identify the *process* factors which 'Help' and 'Hinder' and which have contributed to the success (or otherwise) of the meeting/event and to measure the *Level of Process Maturity* of the group.

When to Use
The Process Iceberg® Review Model is used at the end of a meeting or event.

How to Use
1.   Ask the Group "What has *helped* in terms of the *Objectives* – in achieving the task today?"

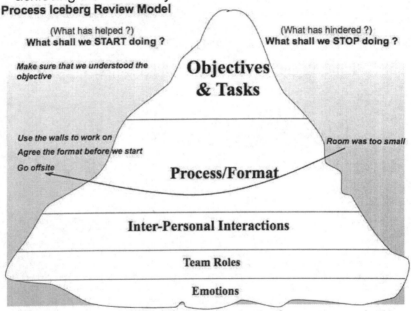

Process Iceberg Review Model

(What has helped ?)
What shall we START doing ?

(What has hindered ?)
What shall we STOP doing ?

Make sure that we understood the objective

Objectives & Tasks

Use the walls to work on

Agree the format before we start

Go offsite

Room was too small

Process/Format

Inter-Personal Interactions

Team Roles

Emotions

2.   When they have identified an aspect of process, ask them "So what will *you do* next time?" When they give the answer, write the statement on the Model *in the appropriate place (on the left hand side). Do NOT put the horizontal lines in until you have collected all the actions for that level.*

3.   Then ask the Group "What else helped?" and when they have identified a process factor, ask them "So what will you do next time?" Write this statement on the Model.

5. Continue to do this, asking the same question *for each level of the Process Iceberg® (Process/Format, Interpersonal Skills, Team Roles)* and write what they have agreed they will do in the appropriate place on the left hand side of the Process Iceberg® Review Model.

6. Then ask "Is there *anything else* that helped?" and ask "What they will do next time?" and write that on the Model.

7. If anyone mentions a 'Symptom' – that is something which is *caused by something else* – *higher up the Process Iceberg®,* (e.g. 'We were much more open today' or 'We shared more'), then ask the Group "What made that happen/possible?" and put the answer in the appropriate place, *higher* up the Process Iceberg®.

8. Finally ask, "What hindered?" and write that on the *right hand* side and then ask "So what will you do next time?" and write that on the *left hand side, in the appropriate place.*

Materials
Flip chart and markers
Process Iceberg® Review Model, on the Flip Chart.

Time
Approximately 15 minutes but it can be much quicker or longer if required.

16. Symptom, Cause, Action (S C A)
(Process Model and Data collection)

Purpose
This process technique is used in conjunction with the Process Iceberg® as a diagnostic tool.

When to Use
This technique can be used at any time to diagnose what is going wrong with the way a group is functioning, to explore causes and to see where corrective action should be taken. It can also be used at an operational and strategic level to audit organisational issues.

How to Use
Group Dynamics
Symptoms - look around at the group and at what is going on. Look at:
- the group dynamics - is there interaction?
- the energy level of the group - is it high, low or neutral?
- the way people are being utilised - is everyone involved (that does not mean everyone talking - some may be thinking!)?
- the process technique - is it giving the results people need?

It is unlikely that the **Symptom** will be any *higher* in the Process Iceberg than this.

Look at your Process Iceberg® and decide where the signs and the symptoms are. Once you have identified the emotion then look *higher* up the Process Iceberg for the **Cause**. This may be that:
- the *Team Roles* are unbalanced, there may be an over-dominance of one or two types or a lack of such roles as creative thinkers or people to direct the process.
- if the group is operating in *Uncertainty* there may be a breakdown in *Interpersonal Skills* such that there are misunderstanding and assumptions being made.
- the *process* or *format* is inappropriate. All kinds of things could be wrong. It could be as simple as: the seating, the lack of flip chart, not displaying things that are said or it could be more serious: the wrong or inappropriate model, tool or technique being used or it is too advanced for the group or possibly it is too 'big' or too 'small' to handle the task.
- the group is unclear about the *Objectives*. The task may be uncertain and the group may have failed to identify the *real* questions/issues.

The Art, Science and Skill of Facilitation

Once you have identified the level, which is causing the problem then decide where to take **Action** as *high* up the Process Iceberg as possible. This would necessitate:

- you injecting 3s and 4s on behalf of the group (4 Level Model of Feedback) at the *Interpersonal Skills* level to clarify (misunderstanding); to 'interpret' for a specialist or to 'translate' between two different personality types (e.g. 'iN' and 'S' in Myers Briggs (see page 44) ; 'Plant' and 'Completer Finisher' in Belbin®).
- undertaking an SPO and suggesting a new/different tool or technique or a different *Format* to help the group.
- encouraging the group to redefine or define the *Objectives* more clearly. (Again use SPO and 3s and 4s to bring clarity of purpose to the group.)

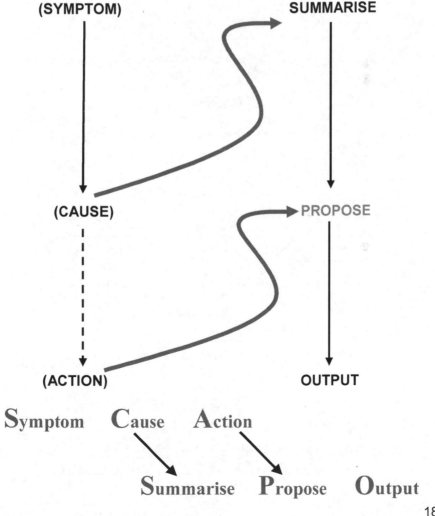

Organisational Issues
Decide which format to use *All; All to One; Group; One to All*

Symptoms
Have Post Its™ and have people write the *symptoms* of the situation on Post Its™. Remember to use different colours and sizes (if appropriate). 'Post' the Post Its™ on a 'back-drop' of a Process Iceberg (see Diagram 1 below) – using the most appropriate format, at the appropriate level on the Iceberg. Wherever they are placed, they will usually be symptoms.

Causes
Then invite people to braindump the cause behind these symptoms. Then to 'post' a different colour Post Its™ on the Iceberg at the appropriate level (see Diagram 2).

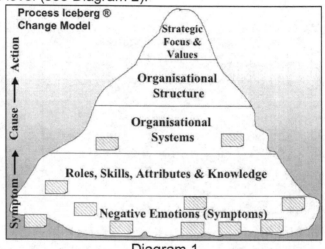

Diagram 1

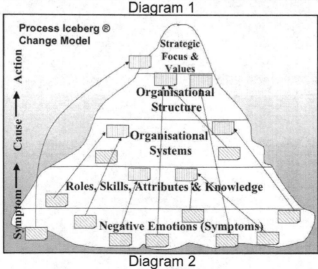

Diagram 2

The Art, Science and Skill of Facilitation

There may be:
- more than one cause of a symptom
- more than one symptom created by one cause

Actions
Then have the group identify *actions* (see Diagram 3)

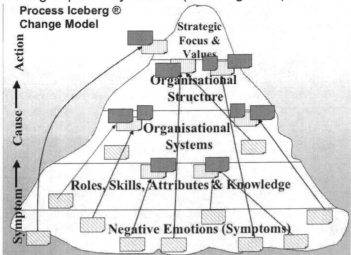

Diagram 3

The group can then:
- decide which actions to focus on (using Dots)
- create action plan (using *Five Questions* – page 170*)*
- explore any forces working for and against the actions (using *Force Field Analysis* - page 173*)*

Materials
Marker pens
White paper
Dots
Post Its™

Time
One hour or more depending on the *Uncertainty* of the issues

Associated Process Tools
Feedback
SPO
Process Iceberg® Model
Force Field
Five Questions

17. Agenda Format
(Process Model)

Purpose
This model (see example on next page) is designed to ensure that meetings are sufficiently prepared. It takes the person who is setting up the meeting/event through a series of questions and prompts the person's thinking.

When to Use
This model should be used for any meeting/event, which is going to require the participants to work through issues, which are uncertain. It is also invaluable when people need to know what is expected of them at the meeting and to ensure that there are no surprises.

How to Use
1. Get everyone who has an Item for the Agenda to provide a short description of that Item and the Objective. The Objective should begin with the word *'To....'* there should be no *'and...'*. This suggests that there is another objective *or* the statement is not the highest-level objective. If the person cannot identify an objective then this is an indication that the issue is *uncertain,* therefore accept the description and explore the objective in the meeting. Remember to leave 4½ times the imagined time to deal with this issue (see next page).

2. The meeting organiser then works through each objective identifying the Tasks/Activities (which will need to take place in order to achieve the Objectives). This should go into as much depth as possible. Avoid the mistake of leaving the Objective at too high a level – it needs to be broken down into the Task steps, which will help achieve the required outcome.

Then these are put in a logical order and the Item defined as:
*   *Certain* (the question is known and the answer is easily identified)
*   *Complex* (the question is known and there will be a number of potential solutions/answers)
*   *Uncertain* (even the question is unclear and will need defining before solutions can be explored).
Note: Although an Objective may be, for example, *complex*, an individual task/activity may be *uncertain.*

3. The first three columns of the Agenda Format (see diagram on next page) are then completed and sent back to the originator who is asked:
*   does it make sense?

The Art, Science and Skill of Facilitation

- will this achieve the Objective?
- will the Item and the Actions generate emotion or will it be neutral?

4. Once the Tasks/Activities and the level of uncertainty has been defined the organiser can discuss the process and format with the facilitator. The facilitator should then select the most appropriate approach to tackle the tasks and choose the models, tools and techniques which will:
- be effective in handling the tasks
- suit the group's level of maturity

Once the facilitator has done this, they should be able to determine how long each Item will take to complete and be able to identify and together with the Task Leader, they can identify the Preparation required.

5. The organiser and the facilitator then decide how many, and which Items should stay on the Agenda based on the time available. They then decide who should carry out the preparation.

6. The Agenda is then issued to the participants.

Objectives	Tasks	Degree of Uncertainty	Process/ Format	Time	Preparation
The objectives -that is, what is the purpose of the meeting. This will in turn cause them to realise the degree of uncertainty raised by the Objective	The sub - tasks ensure that all aspects of the objective get explored. The degree of uncertainty will determine the degree to which the objective is broken down into sub - tasks	The level of uncertainty can then be defined and this will help people to recognise how difficult the task is going to be	Each sub - task may require a different format. The format chosen will depend on: the number of participants; the level of process awareness of the group; the degree of uncertainty and the time available	The time needed for each Stage in the Process so that there is an accurate picture of the total time needed	Finally there may be a need and a benefit that can be gained by undertaking some preparation. This should be identified and individuals tasked with doing it.

Materials
Email can help speed up the process

Time
The process can take several iterations - going backwards and forwards between the 'Item holders', the Task Leader and the facilitator, however, the time spend 'up front' will save a great deal of time at the event and probably prevent the event 'crashing' into emotion.

Associated Process Tools
Feedback Model to ensure understanding of the issues
SPO to develop the Format

Key Process Models, Tools and Techniques

AGENDA FORMAT FOR:　　　　　**DATE:**　　**TIME:**　　**LOCATION:**

OBJECTIVES	TASKS/ ACTIVITIES	CE CO UN[16]	FORMAT	TIME	PREPARATION

[16] CE = Certainty, CO= Complexity and UN= Uncertainty

187

18. Key Driver Analysis - Scenario Planning Methodology
(Strategic Analysis and Implementation)

Purpose
This model is designed to provide a methodology for exploring the external environment and identifying the Key Drivers for change.

When to Use
Regularly, in order to ensure that the organisation is monitoring the factors for change and to prevent the organisation becoming complacent.

How to Use
1. Collect data about the external environment from as many sources as possible. Avoid simply examining the 'close-in' environment and look as wide as possible at the changes going on everywhere.
2. Sort the data into 'themes' which will become the *Key Drivers* (KDs) together with the underpinning *influences* (see Chart 1).
3. Plot the KDs on a 'Likelihood'/Impact four box model and identify the most significant KDs affecting the organisation's future.
4. Write a description of each KD which can be used to explain it to *anyone* else in the organisation (see Chart 2).
5. Either:
   If the *Strategic Goals* are 'set' and relatively immovable (i.e. constrained by legislation or Charter) then go to Chart 3 – *Core Capabilities*. Then identify the *Core Capabilities* needed by the organisation to respond to the Key Drivers (KDs).
   or:
   If the *Capabilities* of the organisation are defined and mandated (i.e. because of legal constraints, legislation, boundaries) then go to Chart 4 – *Strategic Goals*. This will either be re-emphasising the existing strategic (BAU - Business as Usual) goals or be created as new transformational goals (TTB – Transforming the Business). Write a *Strategic Focus* statement which can be used to explain the business to anyone in the organisation.

6. Identify the *Core Values* (see Chart 5), which will underpin the organisation and write an *Ethos Description which* can explain the values to staff, customers and suppliers. Do not forget to identify and integrate *Capabilities,* which will be needed to support the Core Values (Chart 3).

Scenario Planning Model

- Identify Key Drivers
- Define KD Context — Chart 2
- Identify Core Capabilities
- Structure
- Systems
- SAKs — Chart 3
- Strategic Plan for Change
- Define Strategic Scope
- Identify Goals, Objectives & KPIs — Chart 4
- Chart 5 — Identify Values
- Articulate Ethos

The Scenario Planning Questions

Key Drivers

- What are the external Influences on the organisation?
- How do these combine to create the Key Drivers?
- What is the likely Scenario?

Strategic Focus/ Goals

- What is the thrust for future business?
- What is the scope of products / services and markets that WILL and WILL NOT be considered?
- What is the priority and emphasis for products and markets that fall within this scope?

Core Capabilities and Competencies

- What key capabilities are required to make the strategic vision happen?
- What are the 'gaps' in the current capabilities compared with what is required?
- What competencies are needed in the key roles

Core Values

- What are the core values we have at the moment?
- Will the Scenario or Goals require a 'shift' in core values?

Key Process Models, Tools and Techniques

CHART 1
SCENARIO PLANNING – CREATING KEY DRIVER GROUPS

Organisation: Date: ....

KD Group [17]	Key Driver [18]	Impact [19]	Likelihood [20]	Influences [21]

---

[17] Please enter a Category (and ID) for the Key Driver

[18] Enter a *short* description for the Key Driver

[19] Enter a number between '1' and '5' to indicate your view as to the Impact of this Influence/Key Driver on the organisation's future operations/effectiveness – where '1' is *minimal* and '5' is *very significant*

[20] Enter a number between '1' and '5' to indicate your view as to the Likelihood of this Influence/Key Driver happening/coming about – where '1' is *limited likelihood* and '5' is *very likely*

[21] Enter the related Influences for each Key Driver

© *Resource Strategic Change Facilitators*

The Art, Science and Skill of Facilitation

CHART 2
SCENARIO PLANNING – CREATING A SCENARIO CONTEXT

Scenario.................   Date: ....

Category (ID)[22]	Key Driver Group[23]	I	L	Comments[24]

---

[22] Please enter the Key Driver ID
[23] Enter the title of the Key Driver
[24] Enter the description of the Key Driver Group

Key Process Models, Tools and Techniques

Key Driver Context Description[25]:

---

[25] Enter a narrative about the external environment (based on the Key Driver Groups

The Art, Science and Skill of Facilitation

CHART 3
CORE CAPABILITY

Group ID[26]	Core Capability[27]	Importance	Level Required	Gap	Comments

[26] Use PRO1 etc (Processes); STR1 etc (Structure); SYS1 etc (Systems)

[27] These will be: Processes; Structure or Systems

Key Process Models, Tools and Techniques

CHART 4
STRATEGIC FOCUS – GOALS AND OBJECTIVES

Strategy Title:.................   Date:.............

Category (ID)[28]	GOALS[29]	OBJECTIVES[30]

---

[28] Please enter the Goal ID – either TTB1 (Transforming the Business) etc or BAU 1 (Business as Usual)
[29] Enter a title for the Goal
[30] Enter the objectives/make-up of the Goals

The Art, Science and Skill of Facilitation

Strategic Focus Description[31]:

---
[31] Enter a narrative about the Strategic Focus (based on the Goals)

Key Process Models, Tools and Techniques

CHART 5
CORE VALUES[32]

CV No		Need	Impact

---

[32] These should describe the *behaviour(s)* that demonstrates the Value

The Art, Science and Skill of Facilitation

Ethos Description

Applying Format

Applying Format

This is taken from the example on page 3. In Column 2 is the proposed *Format* and in Column 3 is the rationale for selecting each approach. Do not worry if your proposals are different <u>as long as your rationale makes sense.</u>

Objective and Task	Process	Rationale
Objective : To identify cost savings without risk to quality and safety	Someone (*One to All*) says aloud what they think the purpose of the meeting is. This is written on the flip chart and refined as each person speaks until everyone is comfortable with the issue	*This process allows everyone to listen to the perception of others and to build a commonly agreed objective. If there was a complete failure to agree an objective then the team should be broken into Groups to develop a view as to the key issue(s).*
Task 1:		
Identify any areas where savings might be made	Everyone (*All to One*) calls out an area and this is written on the flip chart in column 1 of a matrix, until all potential areas have been captured	*This will avoid focusing on ONE area which was what was disturbing Suchit*
Activities		
1a) Identify aspects of each area where these savings might be made	(*Group*) This might be done in pairs - each pair taking an area, or everyone doing each area in turn. Identify aspects, which could be subject to cost cutting.	*This will avoid a manager 'picking' on someone else's area, but allow another person to challenge narrow self interest)*
1b) Identify the potential savings in monetary terms	This might mean managers going away and doing some research.	*We should avoid the thinking that everything should be done in one meeting – in bread production there is a 'gap' whilst each batch of*

The Art, Science and Skill of Facilitation

	bread is 'proved')
Task 2:	
Measure each saving against the criteria of risk to: quality and customer satisfaction	Someone (*One to All*) then suggests a score for risk against each criteria and everyone challenges or accepts that score. This is done until all the savings have been vetted and an overall risk score is identified.	This saves time and provides an opportunity for those with the specialist knowledge to give their views and opinion.
Task 3:	
Examine any adverse consequences of such cost cutting (other than quality and safety (e.g. low morale)	(*All*) Brainstorming potential adverse consequences. Then combining these in an *All to One*. (*Did you know that as a result of 'speed bumps', the instances of asthma amongst the 'at risk' groups – the young and elderly went up threefold!*).	Allowing maximum participation and engagement and then providing an opportunity to share and see common ideas.
Task 4:	
The manager's should now be able to articulate areas (and aspects) where cuts could be made	Someone (*One to All*) propose which aspects to apply the cuts and come to an agreement.	The Task Leader should be able to summarise on behalf of the group without fear of prejudice or bias.

Matrix for Assessing Group Process Awareness

Behaviour of the Individuals and the Group	0% ⟷ 100%		
	Dys functional	Transitional	Process Aware
Do they use aids, such as flip charts/whiteboards?	✓		
Is there a 'set' leader and does the leader take the key decisions?		✓	
Does everyone sit in the same place; does the group always work in the same room/environment?	✓		
Do they adapt the way they work to suit the task?	✓		
Do they discuss the process?	✓		
Do they review how they work?		✓	
Do individuals take responsibility for the way they behave and contribute?			✓

In this example, the group is predominantly dysfunctional and would need an interventionist style to help develop an understanding of process and introduce tools and techniques which can help them in the future.

The Art, Science and Skill of Facilitation

Agenda Format - "Irregularities" Workshop

Objective	Time	Activity	Format	Preparation
Arrival	08.30 – 09.00	Register	Bacon 'butties' and coffee/tea available on arrival	Bacon 'butties'
	09.00 – 09.15	Introduction and objectives of the day	*Time allocated for Step 1: 10 minutes* **Step 1:** Aileen/Tim outline the day and the various activities and introduces the Facilitator *Time allocated for Step 2: 10 minutes* **Step 2:** Facilitator explains the nature of the activities and how people will be invited to take part and contribute – emphasising that: • Everything will be 'un-attributed' • Everybody's input is valued • You can write/speak or record any key points they want to make • There are no 'wrong' inputs *[Possibly we could have an 'audio booth' where people could go and record, in confidence, any points they want to make about dangerous actions/behaviours which they want people to know about but??]*	Can we have: • 3 flipcharts • 2 roaming mics • 1 podium mic • Name tags • 36 Felt tip pens (three colours) • 24 packs of Post Its™ (one per table and two per Master Class) • 12 tables x 10 people • 1 audio recorder with mic (if possible) • computer projector (and screen)

Agenda Format - "Irregularities" Workshop

				Computer projector?
To take stock of the project so far	09.15 – 09.30	Project update	*Time allocated for Step 1: 15 minutes* **Step 1:** Presentation 1- Presentation by Andy/Ian	
To analyse the *cause*	09.30 – 10.35	Describe the incidents	*Time allocated for Step 1: 20 minutes* **Step 1:** Different people in Geoff's team describe the various incidents (which are displayed on the walls. Geoff feeds back what he understands to be the facts of the incident (but not the cause).	The incidents are written up and displayed on twelve A0 pieces of paper (preferably printed) giving: • a 'title' for the incident • a description of the incident • the location • the time of day/week/ weather conditions • any other pertinent facts (but not *factors*). **A total of 12 incidents are displayed even if**
		Exploring the *cause* of incidents	*Time allocated for Step 2: 30 minutes* **Step 2:** Each table goes to a different incident so that the 12 tables are standing at an incident. The group discuss the incident and are encouraged to think • how the incident could have happened • what were the key factors contributing to the incident • what lessons can be learnt	
		Measure the cause of incidents	The table captures comments and 'an incident facilitator' notes their comments on Post Its™ under each of the headings. *Time allocated for Step 3: 15 minutes*	
		Summarise the cause of incidents		

202

The Art, Science and Skill of Facilitation

				this means duplicating some.
	10.35 – 10.55	Tea/coffee break	**Step 3**: The group cluster their thoughts (with the help of the 'incident facilitator') and draw conclusions under each heading.	
To explore the potential remedies	10.55 – 11.45	*Measure* the *main causes* Explore *potential remedies* Summarise learning	*Time allocated for Step 4: 20 minutes* **Step 4**: The group then discuss and explore potential remedies/actions which could prevent the incident in future. They capture their ideas on the 'wall'. *Time allocated for Step 5: 10 minutes* **Step 5**: The group is then asked to vote individually on the causes which they think contribute most to incidents. They do this by allocating a 'score': Major contribution (5); Medium contribution (3); Minor contribution (1). The group then counts the 'scores' for each cause and identifies the 'Top Three'. *Time allocated for Step 6: 20 minutes* **Step 6**: One person from each incident calls out one key cause and one learning point/remedy in turn. These are captured on the Master Flipchart/computer.	Flip chart paper is placed on the 'wall' for every group. A list of key causes of incidents is draw up. This is displayed when required.
To illustrate Safe	11.45 – 12.15	Safe Possession	*Time allocated for Step 1: 30 minutes* **Step 1**: Presentation by Chris Taunton	

Agenda Format - "Irregularities" Workshop

Possession			
	12.15 – 13.15	Lunch	Over lunch people 'sign-up' for Master Classes (maximum of … per workshop)	**Have sheets with a Title and description of each Master Class and spaces for people to write their names (but only enough to ensure that equal numbers go to each workshop)**
To ensure everyone understands about Protection	13.15 – 14.00	Quiz	*Time allocated for Step 1: 24 minutes* **Step 1:** The 'Question Master' asks each question in turn and gives the tables 2 minutes (per question) to consider the multi-choice or open answer. *Time allocated for Step 2: 6 minutes* **Step 2:** The answer sheets are collected and the Question Master reads out the answers (meanwhile 'scorers' are adding up the scores for each table).	**Have 12 copies of the (blank) Answer Sheet ready with pens** **Have a 'prize' for *each person* on the winning table**
To build expertise in Possession	14.00 – 15.00	Master Classes	*Time allocated for Step 1: 5 minutes* *Step 1:* ***Everyone goes to the chosen Master Class.*** *Time allocated for Step 2: 45 minutes*	**Enough rooms for the Master Classes.** **Two pads of Post**

The Art, Science and Skill of Facilitation

				Its™ in each room
			Step 2: The Master Classes run. *Time allocated for Step 3: 10 minutes* **Step 3:** Everyone in pairs braindumps their thoughts about *issues* affecting 'possession' on Post Its™. These are collected and clustered by the leader of each Master Class and a summary given to Geoff.	
	15.00 – 15.15	(Short) Break for tea/coffee		
To explain the actions which are in the process of being put in place	15.15 15.30	Summary	*Time allocated for Step 1: 5 minutes* **Step 1**: Geoff explains the actions, which have been put in place to remedy the Possession Irregularities, and notices the suggestions and points made during the day.	
To review the day	15.15 – 15.45		Aileen/Tim/Sanjay summarises the day	

Facilitator's Skills, Attributes & Knowledge (Saks)
Self Profile Instruction Sheet

© *Resource* Strategic Change Facilitators

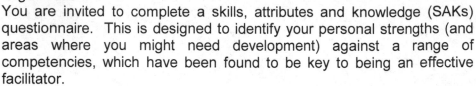

Full name: Email:
Job title: Tel:
Organisation:

You are invited to complete a skills, attributes and knowledge (SAKs) questionnaire. This is designed to identify your personal strengths (and areas where you might need development) against a range of competencies, which have been found to be key to being an effective facilitator.

You will find the 'Self' Questionnaire on the web site at:
http://www.resourceproductions.com/facilitation.html

If you complete the on-line questionnaire you will receive your profile. If you have any problems in completing this questionnaire please contact the address below.

Please answer the questions in the light of your life in general. Do not spend too much time on each question. In completing the questionnaire, you are requested to give careful consideration to the degree to which of each of the statements is true and place a value against each of the questions on the attached questionnaire.

In considering your answers please use the (number) range scale as follows:

7 *Exceptional level of competency* This statement is invariably (almost 100%) true of me.	**3** *Reasonable level of competency* This statement is on occasions (about 25%) true of me.
6 *Very high level of competency* This statement is nearly always (almost 90%) true of me.	**2** *Minimal level of competency* This statement is sometimes (about 10%) true of me.
5 *Good level of competency* This statement is generally (about 75%) true of me.	**1** *Negligible level of competency* This statement is rarely (almost 0%) true of me.
4 *Satisfactory level of competency* This statement is often (about 50%) true of me.	**0** *Unable to comment* I am unable to make a judgement about this.

The Art, Science and Skill of Facilitation

Return to:
Resource
Manna House,
79-79A Norman Lane,
Bradford, BD2 2JX
United Kingdom
Tel: +44 (0) 1274 829003
Fax: +44 (0)1274 635475
www.resourcestrategicchange.com

Facilitation Skills Attributes And Knowledge Questionnaire – Self Perception

(Print) Your Name: ....

ID	Evidence	Score
1	I tend to find that because so much is happening my office is cluttered and things are everywhere	
2	If I was involved in making something happen I have the ability to react quickly to new and unexpected circumstances	
3	I find that I weigh things up quickly and then make a fairly quick, firm decision	
4	I know that I am a person who daydreams and thinks up things on my own	
5	I find that I am quite relaxed even when people reject my suggestions and then find that things go wrong	
6	My ability lies in getting people to make their contribution to the meeting	
7	I find that I prefer to think out loud rather than think things through in my own mind	
8	I avidly watch and listen to the news and current affairs programmes	
9	I tend to make more contributions to the process than I do to the subject matter	
10	I am not a perfectionist and I am not concerned that things are done just right	
11	I have the ability to deal with the unexpected and to see quickly what should be done	
12	I like to think out ways in which our working methods could be changed or improved	
13	I fit in where it is OK to have ideas which are not conventional or ordinary	
14	In my everyday work I hardly ever meet problems that I cannot cope with	
15	I am now more interested in seeing others achieve rather than measuring my own personal success	
16	When I am working on a piece of work I like to bounce it around with others and share my thoughts	
17	I have been known to stop and to get people to look at how we are working together	
18	I am the one who is more likely than others to try something that has not been tried before	

19	If I am trying a new software program on the computer I am happy to dive in and see how it works without necessarily looking at the manual	
20	I prefer situations where I have to react quickly and take the initiative rather than situations where you prepare in detail beforehand	
21	Situations which are familiar and routine make me bored and disinterested	
22	When I have to wait in a queue for something I get more restless and fidgety than most people	
23	When something happens that upsets me, I have the capability to get over it quite easily	
24	I would see myself as a coach rather than a manager	
25	I like it best when there are people around me so that I can interact with them	
26	You can see me in meetings, much more than others, using such things as the flip chart and Post Its™	
27	I have often been known to take a risk by suggesting to a group that they try a different way of doing something	
28	I am the kind of person who enjoys getting the outline and generally scope of something set up but does not relish the detail planning and implementation	
29	If I am in a traffic jam I am the person who will dive off at the next exit and find another way round	
30	My colleagues say that I have the ability to think in an abstract way and to see new ways of doing things	
31	I am comfortable if the plans I have made have to be changed because of other people	
32	When one thing after another goes wrong I tend to be able to go on as usual	
33	My ability lies in helping others give of their best rather than concentrating on my performance	
34	My colleagues would say that I have a broad business knowledge and use it to draw analogies which help people to see things in a new way	
35	People comment that my contributions to a meeting are more to do with the process than the agenda items	
36	In a meeting I am never afraid to suggest that the group try a completely different way of tackling the task	
37	I tend to leave some things to chance rather than make complex plans about every detail	
38	I am the type of person who questions and challenges methods which are seen by others as satisfactory	

39	I know that I am not always practical because I am thinking about things in a conceptual way	
40	I have the ability to be patient with all kinds and types of people	
41	I usually find that I am satisfied with how the day has gone and I have few regrets	
42	I see my future as a facilitator rather more than as a specialist or general manager	
43	I keep abreast of current affairs and what is going on in the country and world	
44	In meetings I find myself concentrating more on how we are tackling something than on the subject itself	
45	If I thought of a different way of approaching an issue in a meeting I would not hesitate to suggest it even if I might look foolish	
46	When I take on a task I would rather just see how it developed rather than make detailed plans	
47	I tend to believe that I am more interested in seeking personal meaning to life than to having a secure job that pays well	
48	I have ideas about all sorts of things, too many to put into practice	
49	If people interrupt me when I am doing something it does not concern me, I take it as it comes	
50	I tend not to get upset at little things and find that I can bounce back easily from disappointments	
51	I would prefer to have lunch with a group of people than on my own and I would be the one talking	
52	I am able to draw examples from a wide range of situations and use them to draw parallels	
53	My interest tends to be on the process in our discussions rather than the topic	
54	I have often been prepared to suggest a different way of doing something even if I was not sure if it might work but I thought it would help	
55	I have the ability to change my plans and to adjust very quickly to a new situation	
56	I like to try to think of new methods of doing tasks when confronted with them, rather than use well tried approaches	
57	Sometimes I know my thoughts are too deep and complicated for many people to understand	
58	I find it easy enough to accept criticism	

59	I tend to share the rationale for an approach because I want the group to understand the connection between the task and the mode/ tool/technique	
60	In building something or working on something I would rather work with other people than on my own	
61	I have the ability to use examples from other organisations to explain our situation	

Produced using **ADaPT®*ability***

FACILITATOR'S SKILLS, ATTRIBUTES & KNOWLEDGE (SAKs) 360° PROFILE INSTRUCTION SHEET

© *Resource* Strategic Change Facilitators

To (Colleague):   From (your name): _____

Date:

Dear

I would be grateful if you would complete a *Facilitator's* questionnaire about me. This is designed to identify my profile measured against a range of competencies. After you have read the instructions below, please complete the questionnaire and return it to:
Resource at the address on the next page.

Your individual responses will remain confidential If you have any problems in completing this questionnaire please contact me.

Please answer the questions in the light of your experience of me. Do not spend too much time on each question. In completing the questionnaire, you are requested to give consideration to the degree to which of each of the statements is true and place a value against each of the questions on the attached questionnaire.

In considering your answers please use the (number) range scale as follows:

7 *Exceptional level of competency* This statement is invariably (almost 100%) true of them.	**3** *Reasonable level of competency* This statement is on occasions (about 25%) true of them.
6 *Very high level of competency* This statement is nearly always (almost 90%) true of them.	**2** *Minimal level of competency* This statement is sometimes (about 10%) true of them.
5 *Frequently relates/refers to Good level of competency* This statement is generally (about 75%) true of you.	**1** *Negligible level of competency* This statement is rarely (almost 0%) true of them.
4 *Satisfactory level of competency* This statement is often (about 50%) true of them.	**0** *Unable to comment* I am unable to make a judgement about this.

212

The Art, Science and Skill of Facilitation

Thank you.

Signed:

Return to:
Resource Strategic Change Facilitators,
Manna House,
79-79A Norman Lane,
Bradford, BD2 2JX
United Kingdom
Tel: +44 (0) 1274 829003
Fax: +44 (0)1274 635475
www.resourcestrategicchange.com

Facilitation Skills Attributes And Knowledge
Questionnaire - Others

(Print) Name of Person being profiled:

_ _

Please indicate (with a cross, '**X**', in the square box) which of the following you are completing the Questionnaire **about**:

My Peer/Colleague ☐

My 'Boss' ☐   My Junior/Direct Report ☐

ID	Evidence	Score
1	They tend to find that because so much is happening their office space is cluttered and things are everywhere	
2	If they am involved in making something happen they have the ability to react quickly to new and unexpected circumstances	
3	They weigh things up quickly and then make a fairly quick, firm decision	
4	They are a person who daydreams and thinks up things on their own	
5	They are quite relaxed even when people reject their suggestions and then find that things go wrong	
6	Their ability lies in getting people to make a personal contribution to the meeting	
7	They prefer to think out loud rather than think things through in their own mind	
8	They avidly watch and listen to the news and current affairs programmes	
9	They tend to make more far more contributions to the process than they do to the subject matter	
10	They are not a perfectionist and they are not concerned that things are done just right	
11	They have the ability to deal with the unexpected and to see quickly what should be done	
12	They like to think out ways in which the group's working methods could be changed or improved	
13	They fit in where it is OK to have ideas which are not conventional or ordinary	
14	In their everyday work they hardly ever meet problems that they cannot cope with	

15	They are now more interested in seeing others achieve rather than measuring their own personal success	
16	When they are working on a piece of work they like to bounce it around with others and share their thoughts	
17	They are best known as someone who will stop and get people to look at how they are working together	
18	They are the one who is more likely than others to try something that has not been tried before	
19	If they were trying a new software program on the computer they would be happy to dive in and see how it works without necessarily looking at the manual	
20	They prefer situations where they have to react quickly and take the initiative rather than situations where they have prepared in detail beforehand	
21	Situations which are familiar and routine make them bored and disinterested	
22	When they had to wait in a queue for something they would get more restless and fidgety than most people	
23	When something happens that upsets them, they have the capability to get over it quite easily	
24	They would see themselves as a 'coach' rather than a (line) manager	
25	They like it best when there are people around me so that they can interact with them	
26	You can see them in meetings, much more than others, using a wide variety of techniques, tools and models to help the group tackle the task	
27	They have often been known to take a risk by suggesting to a group that they try a different way of doing something	
28	They are the kind of person who enjoys getting the outline and generally scope of something set up but does not relish the detail planning and implementation	
29	If they were in a traffic jam they are the type of person who will dive off at the next exit and find another way round	
30	They have the ability to think in an abstract way and to see new ways of doing things	
31	They are comfortable if the plans they have made have to be changed because of other people	
32	When one thing after another goes wrong they tend to be able to go on as usual	
33	Their ability lies in helping others give of their best rather than concentrating on their own performance	

34	They have a broad business knowledge and use it to draw analogies which help people to see things in a new way	
35	People comment that their contributions to a meeting are pitched at the right level for the (process) maturity of the group	
36	In a meeting they are never afraid to suggest that the group try a completely different way of tackling the task	
37	They tend to leave some things to chance rather than make complex plans about every detail	
38	They are the type of person who questions and challenges methods which are seen by others as satisfactory	
39	They know that they are not always practical because they are thinking about things in a conceptual way	
40	They have the ability to be patient with all kinds and types of people	
41	They are satisfied with how the day has gone and have few regrets	
42	They see their future as a facilitator rather more than as a specialist or general manager	
43	They keep abreast of current affairs and what is going on in the country and world	
44	In meetings they concentrate as least as much on how the group is going to tackle the next stage as the present subject matter	
45	If they thought of a different way of approaching an issue in a meeting they would not hesitate to suggest it even if they might look foolish	
46	When they take on a task they would rather just see how it developed rather than make detailed plans	
47	They are more interested in seeking personal meaning to life than to having a secure job that pays well	
48	They have ideas about all sorts of things, too many to put into practice	
49	If people interrupt them when they are doing something, it does not concern them, they take it as it comes	
50	They tend not to get upset at little things and find that they can bounce back easily from disappointments	
51	They would prefer to have lunch with a group of people than on their own and they would be the one interacting	

52	They are able to draw examples from a wide range of situations and use them to draw parallels	
53	Their interest tends to be on the process in any discussion rather than the topic	
54	They have often been prepared to suggest a different way of doing something even if they were not sure if it might work but they thought it would help	
55	They have the ability to change their plans and to adjust very quickly to a new situation	
56	They like to try to think of new methods of doing tasks when confronted with them, rather than use well tried approaches	
57	Sometimes their thoughts are too deep and complicated for many people to understand	
58	They find it easy enough to accept criticism	
59	They share the rationale for the approach that they are suggesting because they want the group to understand for themselves the connection between the task and the mode/l tool/technique	
60	In building something or working on something they would rather work with other people than on their own	
61	They have the ability to use examples from other organisations to explain the current situation facing a group	

Produced using **ADaPT®ability**

Comparison of Models, Tools and Techniques in this Book and associated Manual

Below is a list of the Models, Tools and techniques in this book and the accompanying manual: *"Facilitation - Models, Tools and Techniques for Effective Group Work"[33]*.

Key:
M = Model
T = Tool
Te = Technique

Book	Handbook
Feedback Model (M)	Feedback Model (M)
Analogy (Te)	Analogy (Te)
SPO (T)	SPO (Te)
SCA (M)	SCA (T)
Four Box Model (T)	Four Box Model (T)
Matrix charting (T)	Matrix charting (T)
	Yes …and (Te)
	Out of the Box (Te)
	Braindumping (Te)
	Brainstorming (Te)
	Clustering (Te)
	Linking (Te)
	"Snap" (Te)
	Data Collection (T)
	Flow Charting (M)
Allegory – A Day at the Zoo (T)	
Repertory Grid (M)	
Re-statement (T)	
What will I see happening (T)	What will I see happening (T)
Storytelling (T)	
Is and Is Not (M)	Is and Is Not (M)
	Perceiving others (T)
	Expert Witness (Te)
	Relative Importance Grid (T)
	Going Dotty (Te)

---

[33] ISBN 978-0-9556435-1-4 written by the same author and published by RP Publishing House.

	Essential and Desirable (Te)
	Fishbone (T)
Debate	
Five Questions (T)	Five Questions (T)
Force Field Analysis (M)	Force Field Analysis (T)
Process Iceberg Model (M)	
Agenda Format (M)	
Scenario Planning (M)	
	Moving out from the Centre (Te)
	'Twirly' – Getting out of Orbit (Te)
	Stakeholder Mapping (T)
	Trust and Agreement (T)
	Presentation and Questions (Te)
	Solve™ - Problem Solving and Solution Finding Model (M)
	Defining the Level of Improvement/Change Project (T)
	Commitment Matrix (T)
18 Models, Tools and Techniques	**33 Models, Tools and Techniques**
Unique to Book: 8 Models, Tools and Techniques	**Unique to Manual: 23 Models, Tools and Techniques**
Overall, in the two publications combined there are **31** different **Models, Tools and Techniques.**	

The Handbook shows managers how to be more effective by using a 'facilitative style' when working with groups. The Handbook contains a whole range of models, tools, techniques designed for meetings and project work and team interactions.

As such, the Handbook provides a Facilitator with a compendium of different models, tools and techniques, which should be in their tool bag.

Index